The Hampshire Cookbook

First published in the UK by HCR Ltd

ISBN 978-0-9927524-1-5

Published by HCR Ltd 2013

For more copies of this book, please email: info@hcr.co.uk

Tel: +44 1256 812700

Designed by Dean Chillmaid @ Spacehopper Design
www.spacehopperdesign.co.uk

Printed and bound in Great Britain at
Tyson Press
Printers of fine journals, books and catalogues
Gainsborough House
81 Oxford Street
London
W1D 2EU

I grew up in Hampshire. My dad was a market trader and regularly brought home incredibly exciting ingredients - many of which arrived at Southampton Docks from exotic countries across the globe. I was fascinated with all kinds of food from a very early age.

My appreciation for locally grown produce didn't kick in until I started to learn my trade. But, from the moment I tasted food from my local surroundings in Hampshire, I became hooked.

Even now, I celebrate and use ingredients grown close to my own restaurants. I am lucky enough to be able to use supplies grown on my own farm, just a stone's throw from L'Enclume. Sadly, I am no longer based in Hampshire - I only get to really appreciate the joys of its local produce when I return home to see family and friends.

So, I am delighted to be able to join in this celebration of all that is great about the food produced in my home county - you might say I was made in Hampshire and I am tremendously proud of that.

The Hampshire Cookbook is being published to raise funds for The Prince's Trust - to help disadvantaged young people across the UK enjoy a brighter future. I fully support this worthy cause and hope you enjoy the delicious results of some very hard work from the team of volunteers at HCR.

Simon Rogan
L'Enclume

Contents

18

50

52

108

88

5

MILLION MAKERS

Prince's Trust

Million Makers is an entrepreneurial competition that challenges teams from different corporations to raise as much money as they can, through enterprising initiatives. Teams work together to turn £1500 into £10,000 or more for The Prince's Trust over the course of six months, competing against each other to run the most profitable mini enterprise.

The competition is all about innovation. We ask our Million Makers teams to think beyond cake stalls and fun runs but use their skills, abilities and imagination to create novel, creative ways of raising money.

This year team "Brotherhood" have achieved this goal by creating their very own cookbook, inspired by the produce and dishes of Hampshire.

The funds raised will directly change the lives of disadvantaged young people in the UK. 87p of every pound donated to The Prince's Trust to support our programmes. We give practical and financial support to disadvantaged young people, developing key workplace skills such as confidence and motivation. We work with 13 to 30-year-olds who have struggled at school, have been in care, are long-term unemployed or have been in trouble with the law.

The Prince's Trust offers a range of personal development and vocational programmes, all allied with support from the beginning to the end and beyond, whenever the individual has achieved their goal. We aim to support over 60,000 young people in 2014 and could not do this without the generous support of our corporate partners such as HCR and the fantastic team "Brotherhood".

Gina Moffat

When Gina was sent to Holloway for drug offences at the age of 25, she thought her world had fallen apart. However, things started to change for Gina when, while still in prison, she signed up for an NVQ in floristry. She had always been interested in flowers and knew that getting a qualification would help her make a better life for herself and her daughters.

After the course, Gina spotted a business opportunity and persuaded the prison governor to let her provide floral arrangements for prisoners, visitors and staff. News of its success spread and by the time of her release in 2008, Gina felt confident enough to set up on her own.

However, the reality of setting up a business in the outside world was harder than Gina first expected and she turned to The Prince's Trust for help. The Trust helped Gina to write a business plan, obtain a start-up loan and find subsidised premises in which to work from.

Gina launched "Blooming Scent" at the Bernie Grant Arts Centre in Tottenham, providing flowers and floral decorations for people and events. Gina then decided to expand into catering and snap up a small cafe that had become available at the Centre, following advice from Dragon's Den star and Prince's Trust ambassador James Caan who met with Gina as part of a Prince's Trust event. In September 2013 Gina opened her second cafe, "Blooming Scent at 639" at 639 Tottenham High Road.

Now that she has successfully turned her life around, Gina is determined to help other young people. She has taken on staff in her cafe and likes to help those in need of a second chance – as she once was.

Gina is also now working as a Job Ambassador for The Prince's Trust. Job Ambassadors work in the community helping unemployed young people to find training, education and job opportunities.

A word from our sponsors

FULLER'S
CHISWICK
INDEPENDENT FAMILY BREWERS
ESTD 1845
GRIFFIN BREWERY

Fuller's are delighted to support The Prince's Trust Million Makers in partnership with The Hampshire Cookbook. Being able to combine our passion for great food, local ingredients and our strong Hampshire connection in support of such a worthwhile charity is a fantastic opportunity.

From our people to our produce, we strive for the very best and are proud to support our local communities. As Head of Food for Fuller's Inns, I'm passionate about sourcing the best ingredients and champion our local sourcing ethic and quality, hand-picking suppliers whenever I can. Take the highly reputable Owton's butchers of Chalcroft Farm. The Fuller's food team and I work closely with Billy Owton to source and create unique products to showcase on our menus. Our 28 day, dry-aged cuts of steak and the delicious, hand-crafted, 100% Hampshire beef burgers are a testament to Owton's premium reared cattle and are available throughout our pub estate. This close relationship with our famers and the rest of our supply chain is crucial in ensuring we source our ingredients at their absolute best. As a company we encourage our Pubs to operate as individual businesses and my team and I support them to create quality, freshly prepared menus, bespoke to each and every one. Our chefs are guided by the seasons and you will see this reflected in our menus and daily chalk boards. We've also worked hard to create our own unique, "Only at Fuller's" products which are now available throughout Hampshire and further afield. We incorporate our own beers in many of these dishes; others are simply derived from my age old recipe book!

We hope you enjoy this small snapshot of Chef's recipes from a handful of our superb Hampshire food destinations. I would love to see you in one of our pubs soon to try some of them out!

Paul Dickinson, Head of Food

Look out for...

- Fuller's Hampshire Black Pudding
- Made of Hampshire Ice Cream
- HSB Pork Sausage (That's Horndean Special Bitter, our Gales brew)
- Cranberry & Chestnut Christmas Stuffing"
- London Porter Smoked Salmon" (see recipe on page 38)

Delicious, Sustainable, Ingredients From The Hampshire

Where our food comes from and its traceability has become a hot topic this year and the Hampshire Farmers' Markets (HFM) are finding that more and more people are visiting their markets across Hampshire, to find good quality local produce to cook up all of their favourite recipes.

Each Hampshire Farmers' Market sells a broad range of local, in season produce which has to have been grown, reared, caught, brewed, pickled, baked, or processed in the county or within ten miles of the border. The huge array of delightful and delicious food on offer at each market can include cheeses, meat, poultry, game, fish, fresh fruit and vegetables, eggs, cakes, artisan breads, pastries, vegetarian food, honey, preserves, chutneys, relishes, chilli jams, sauces, rapeseed oil,

dairy produce, goat produce, fruit juices, mead, wine, beer, cider, lavender, soaps, dog treats, wood products and seasonal plants.

Visiting one of the markets is a great way to spend some weekend time, where you can stroll around the stalls, chat to the producers, sample delicious and nutritious fresh food and enjoy the aromas of produce being cooked – savour the delights of an early morning breakfast bap, some home-made cake, fresh croissant, water buffalo burger, hog roast, fruit or some of our award winning cheese and so much more!

You will also discover new and interesting produce that you will not find in the supermarkets, that is beautifully displayed and generally packaging free – another way to help preserve the environment.

Traceable
Farmers' Markets

Regular HFM Food Comparison Survey's clearly demonstrate that a large proportion of the produce is actually cheaper than the supermarkets, with the savings in food miles and also the middle man costs, passed onto customers.

Come and visit one of the regular HFM markets across Hampshire at Alton, Andover, Cosham, Elvetham Heath, Emsworth, Petersfield, Romsey, Southsea and Winchester.

www.hampshirefarmersmarkets.co.uk

Supporting Hampshire's Local Producers

Hampshire Fare, the county food group, Hampshire Fare has been working closely with local farmers and producers for more than twenty years.

Hampshire boasts a thriving local food culture offering award-winning cheeses, meat, vegetables, wine, beer and much more. With so much exceptional local produce on offer Hampshire Fare is passionate about encouraging people to buy locally and discover more about the food and drink on our doorstep.

The free Hampshire Fare Guide to Local Produce, Food, Drink and Crafts will help you to discover where you can try and buy local produce. Pick up a copy from your local Tourism Information Centre or download from the Hampshire Fare website.

Be the first to hear about local food and drink news, events, offers and competitions by signing up for the free monthly Hampshire Fare e-newsletter.

If you are making or serving local produce and would like to benefit from all that we can offer you as a producer or hospitality member contact Tracy Nash on 01962 845999 or tracy. nash@hampshirefare.co.uk. www.hampshirefare.co.uk*

Hampshire Charcuterie

Delicious Hampshire Charcuterie products are now being made locally as a result of a two-year project led by Hampshire Fare and funded by The Prince's Countryside Fund.

Hampshire Fare recognised the challenges being faced by pig farmers. Increasing feed prices and no European or state funding meant that making money from pig farming was proving impossible for many Hampshire Farmers.

Hampshire Fare gave local producers the opportunity to become skilled in the art of charcuterie making. After

two years of hard work a group of local producers and butchers are now offering a range of Hampshire Charcuterie which enables the producers to add value to their meat.

The project has received a lot of attention including an invitation to Clarence House to celebrate The Prince's Countryside Fund and the people it supports.

Hampshire Charcuterie is available directly from the producers and can also be found at many local food events. Discover more: www.hampshirecharcuterie.co.uk

Image: L-R HRH The Prince of Wales, Sarah Mills from Parsonage Farm, Tracy Nash from Hampshire Fare and Martin Martindale from Greenfield Pork Products.

Simon Rogan

Praised for his technical brilliance and renowned for his use of unusual ingredients, combinations, styles and blending of tastes and textures, Simon Rogan has been called "one of the most innovative chefs in the country" by the Guardian, and his restaurants – L'Enclume and Roganic – are known for producing some of the most startlingly original menus around.

Ingredients

For the cod mousse
- 233g salted cod, rinsed
- 200g whipping cream
- 87g potato puree
- 1 leaf of gelatine

For the yolk gel
- 500ml vegetable stock
- 50g whipping cream
- 0.5g saffron
- 30g vege gel

For the sage cream
- 250g sage oil
- 3 yolks
- 2 eggs
- 5g salt
- 5g sherry vinegar
- 7g Dijon mustard

For the salt and vinegar rice
- 100g wild rice
- Vinegar powder
- Salt
- Tapioca maltodextrin

To garnish
- Green pea shoot
- Golden pea shoot
- Rape seed oil

Cod Yolk, Sage Cream And Pea Shoots, Salt And Vinegar Rice

Serves: 6

Method

For the cod mousse
Bloom the gelatine in cold water. Seal the cod in a bag at full pressure, cook in a water bath at 50°C for 15 minutes. Bring cream to the boil, heat potato puree. Put all hot into a blender, add the gelatine and blitz to a smooth consistency. Allow to cool, then pipe into moulds and freeze.

For the yolk gel
Place the veg stock, cream and saffron in a pan and bring to a simmer, take off the heat & cool. Then pass through a fine sieve, add the vege gel and return to heat, bring to the boil while stirring. Keep warm.

For dipping the yolks
Take the frozen cod mousse hemi spheres and push a cocktail stick into each one at an angle. Ensuring the saffron gel is kept at 70°C, dip each hemi sphere into the gel twice, in succession and reserve in an ovenproof dish with the cocktail stick still in place, defrost in a fridge.

For the sage cream
Place the yolks, eggs, salt, vinegar and mustard in a Thermomix and blend together, slowly add the sage oil, while blending to make a sage mayonnaise. Add this to a cream whipper and charge twice, place the whipper in a water bath at 50°C and reserve.

For the salt and vinegar rice
Heat vegetable oil to 220°C and fry the wild rice until it puffs, drain onto paper towel and cool. Put the puffed wild rice into a bowl & season with vinegar powder and salt. Add tapioca maltodextrin until you have the desired consistency.

To serve
Take the yolks, cover with cling film and heat at 50°C in a hot cupboard. Place a spoonful of salt and vinegar rice in a bowl, place a cod yolk on top, twisting out the cocktail stick, garnish with the pea shoots. Cover one side of the yolk where the cocktail stick was with the sage cream and finish with rape seed oil.

Rick Stein

Rick Stein OBE is a chef, restaurateur, cookery book author and television presenter. He has written 19 cookery books, an autobiography and made 25 cookery programmes. He has also cooked for The Queen and Prince Philip, Tony Blair, Margaret Thatcher and French President, Jacques Chirac. Rick is best known for a love of fresh seafood and made his name in the 90's with his earliest books and television series based on his life as chef and owner of The Seafood Restaurant in fishing port of Padstow on the North Coast of Cornwall. As he said at the time "nothing is more exhilarating than fresh fish simply cooked." Since then he has expanded his horizons to cover numerous journeys over the world in search of great dishes, many of which he's brought back to his restaurants in Padstow. His current television series Rick Stein's Indian Odyssey and cookery book, Rick Stein's India, embarks on a spectacular journey through the Indian sub-continent in search of recipe inspiration and the perfect curry. Eager to introduce new curries to British taste buds, he travels to Kolkata (Calcutta) to experience its ethnic influences, discovers the temple food of Tamil Nadu and house-boat hospitality in Kerala, explores India's gourmet state - The Punjab, and tastes the regal cooking of Rajasthan, unearthing new flavours and dishes along the way. In September 2013, Rick released his memoirs, Under a Mackerel Sky.

Ingredients

- 1 kg mussels
- 30 ml dry white wine
- 60 g tomatoes, peeled, deseeded and finely chopped
- 5 g French tarragon, finely chopped
- 30 ml extra virgin olive oil
- 2 cloves garlic, finely chopped
- 30 g unsalted butter

Steamed Mussels with Tomato and Tarragon

Method

1. Make sure the mussels are tightly closed. If they are fresh-farmed ones there is no need to wash them, but if they are showing any signs of grit or sand wash them in copious amounts of cold water.

2. Take a large saucepan, add the olive oil and garlic and soften over a medium heat for about a minute. Add the mussels, turn up the heat and add the white wine. Put a lid on the pan and cook for a few minutes until all the shells have opened, but only just. Stir the shells once or twice during the cooking to distribute them evenly. Remove and pour through a colander set over a bowl.

3. Keep the mussels warm while you transfer the liquor to a pan, heat until boiling, whisk in the butter then add the tomato and tarragon. Check the seasoning; it's always a good idea to leave seasoning to the end with shellfish because you never know how salty they are going to be, then add salt if necessary and freshly ground black pepper.

4. Add the mussels back into the pan. Serve with plenty of crusty bread or alternatively with a mound of al dente linguine pasta.

© CRAIG EASTON OF DRIFTWOOD DESIGNS

Tommy Miah

Entrepreneur and Celebrity Chef Tommy Miah is one of the leading Bangladeshi businessmen in the UK where he owns the award-winning Raj Restaurant in Edinburgh. He is the founder and promoter of the International Indian Chef of the Year Competition: the most prestigious event in the Indian culinary calendar, attracting 5000 entrants – both amateur and professional – from all corners of the world.

Tommy Miah returns regularly to Bangladesh where he has diverse business interests and commitments including his signature restaurant The Heritage - the home of his original bangla-fusion style of cooking and fine dining.

Drawing upon his status as a media celebrity and TV chef, coupled with wide experience of international dining and catering, has resulted in the foundation of the Tommy Miah Institute of Hospitality Management to train young Bangladeshis and equip them to succeed in the international hospitality industry. The recipe below is the winning dish from the Tommy Miah's International Indian Chef of the Year Competition. The competition was set up to help charities and helps promote chefs to achieve their goals.

Ingredients

- 2 1/2 pounds chicken thighs with bone, skin discarded
- 4 medium shallots, quartered
- 5 garlic cloves, chopped
- 1 tablespoon minced peeled ginger
- 2 sprigs fresh curry leaves, leaves removed from stems
- 1 teaspoon cayenne
- 1/4 teaspoon black peppercorns
- 10 whole cloves
- (1-inch) piece cinnamon stick
- 1 teaspoon distilled white vinegar
- 1/2 cup water
- About 2 cups vegetable oi
- 1 medium onion, thinly sliced
- 3 teaspoons all-purpose flour, divided

Aromatic Chicken

Method

1. Toss all ingredients except water, oil, onion, and flour with 1 teaspoon salt in a wide heavy medium pot. Marinate chicken, covered and chilled, 1 hour.

2. Add water and bring to a boil, then simmer, covered, until chicken is tender, 40 minutes to 1 hour.

3. Meanwhile, heat 1 1/2 inches oil in a small heavy saucepan over medium heat until hot but not smoking. Toss onion with 1 teaspoon flour, then fry in 2 batches, stirring frequently (do not let burn), until golden brown, 2 to 3 minutes per batch. Transfer with a slotted spoon to paper towels. Reserve 3 tablespoons oil.

4. Remove chicken from cooking liquid, reserving liquid, and gently pat dry. 3Heat reserved oil in a 12-inch heavy skillet over medium-high heat until it shimmers, then brown chicken all over, about 6 minutes total. Transfer to a platter.

5. Add remaining 2 teaspoons flour to fat in skillet and cook, stirring, 1 minute. Add chicken-cooking liquid (with aromatics and spices) and simmer, stirring, until slightly thickened, about 2 minutes. Season with salt and pour over chicken. Top with fried onions.

Green Bengal Coconut Fish Curry
Method

1. Heat the oil in a non-stick pan, add the mustard seeds, cloves, cardamom pods and cinnamon stick and stir fry for 20 seconds (be careful, the seeds might pop). Add half of the chopped onion and fry for 4-5 minutes until soft.

2. Meanwhile, place the remaining onion, the ginger, garlic, ground coriander and 100ml/3½fl oz of the coconut milk into a blender or food processor and blend to a smooth purée.

3. Add this mixture to pan along with the whole green chillies and salt, to taste. Cover with a lid and cook over a low heat for 12-15 minutes, giving the pot an occasional stir.

4. Add the remaining coconut milk, the water, the curry leaves, black pepper and garam masala and the fish and leave to cook undisturbed for about 3-5 minutes, until the fish is opaque and cooked through.

Ingredients

- 2 tbsp vegetable oil
- ½ tsp brown mustard seeds
- 4 cloves
- 6 green cardamom pods, lightly crushed
- 1 large piece cinnamon stick
- 1 small onion, finely chopped
- 5cm/2in piece fresh ginger, peeled and quartered
- 2 large garlic cloves
- 1 tsp ground coriander
- 300ml/10½fl oz coconut milk
- 2-4 green chillies, left whole
- Salt, to taste
- 100ml/3½fl oz water
- 10 curry leaves
- ½-1 tsp freshly ground black pepper
- ¾ tsp garam masala
- 500g/1lb 2oz salmon or firm white fish fillets, cut into large pieces

Marcus Wareing

Lancashire-born Marcus Wareing's early years as a chef were spent in the kitchens of The Savoy, Le Gavroche, and La Tante Claire, which gave him a firm grounding in classical French cooking. When Wareing worked alongside Gordon Ramsay at Le Gavroche, In 1993, Wareing helped Ramsay to launch Aubergine, before becoming head chef at his mentor's L'Oranger restaurant – where he won his first Michelin.

Three years later, Wareing headed up the original Pétrus, followed by the Savoy Grill & Banquette. Wareing earned a Michelin star at Savoy Grill and two at Pétrus. In 2009, Wareing was named Chef of the Year by both GQ magazine and the AA Restaurant Guide. Two years later, he opened his second restaurant, The Gilbert Scott, in the painstakingly refurbished St Pancras Renaissance Hotel.

Ingredients

- Pork chops
- 1 rack of pork short ribs
- 1l of apple juice
- 1 knob of fresh ginger
- 1 red chilli
- 2 shallots
- 2 garlic cloves
- 1/2 tsp of coriander seeds
- 1 star anise
- 1 cinnamon stick
- 1 tsp of allspice powder
- 1 tbsp of peppercorns

Barbecue sauce
- 140g of ketchup
- 1 tsp of black treacle
- 1 tsp of Worcestershire sauce
- 1 tbsp of wholegrain mustard
- 1/2 tsp of sweet smoked paprika
- 1/2 tsp of hot smoked paprika
- 1 dash of Tabasco
- 1/2 lemon, juiced
- 1 garlic clove, finely chopped
- 1 pinch of salt
- Freshly ground black pepper

Apple purée
- 2 Braeburn apples
- 2 tbsp of honey
- 3 sprigs of lemon thyme, leaves picked
- 1 tbsp of vegetable oil

Endive
- 2 white endive
- 100ml of Knorr Chicken stock
- 1 knob of butter

Pork Chops and Ribs

Method

1. Take 4 pork chops, brined in a 5% brine, for one hour.

2. Begin this barbecue pork recipe by making the sauce. For the barbecue sauce, combine all the ingredients together and mix well. Set aside.

3. For the apple purée, preheat the oven to 165°C/gas mark 3.5. Cut the apples into quarters and lay on a baking tray, cover with the honey, lemon thyme and oil. Place the baking tray in the oven and cook until the apples are golden.

4. Transfer the apples to a blender and blend into a purée. Pass through a fine sieve and set aside in the fridge.

5 For the ribs, place all the spices, peppercorns, shallot, garlic and apple juice in a pan. Bring to the boil. Once boiling, reduce to a gentle simmer and add the ribs. Cover and cook over a low heat until the meat is tender, approximately 2 hours.

6. Once the meat is tender, remove from the stock and set aside. Bring the stock to the boil and reduce to the consistency of a syrup, add to the barbecue sauce.

7. Cut the ribs into single bones and use a pastry brush to coat the bones in the barbecue sauce. Set aside.

8 Preheat the oven to 180°C/ gas mark 4. Cut the endive into quarters lengthways and sear in a pan with a knob of butter until well coloured. Add the chicken stock and transfer to the oven and cook for 6-8 minutes or until tender, do not turn the oven off.

9 Heat a grill or light a barbecue. Season the pork chops with salt and pepper and grill on both sides until golden brown all over, the chops are best served slightly pink in the middle. Allow to rest.

10 Warm the ribs in the oven along with the apple purée. Serve the ribs and apple purée with the grilled pork chops and endive.

25

Antonio Carluccio

The warm infectious Antonio Carluccio was given the national honour of Commendatore dell' Ordine al Merito della Repubblica Italiana by the Italian government, the equivalent to a British knighthood, in 1998 for his contribution to the Italian food industry, and in 2007 he was awarded an OBE. His Italian based dishes evoke memories of his childhood and are enjoyed by thousands in his self-titled restaurants, of which there are over 70 in the UK. Perhaps along with risotto with truffles, risotto with ceps is the best-known of Italian rice dishes. Italians eat this only in season when the porcino is around, but the following recipe he has devised will enable you to enjoy a mushroom risotto throughout the year. Should you manage to find some fresh porcini, however, Antonio urges you to try them, the taste is sensational! Antonio also chose a mushroom risotto as he goes foraging in Hampshire.

Ingredients

- 2 litres chicken or vegetable stock
- 4 tbsp olive oil or, 50g unsalted butter
- 1 onion, peeled and very finely chopped
- 300g firm button mushrooms, finely sliced
- 50g dried porcini (ceps), rehydrated and chopped
- 350g carnaroli or arborio risotto rice
- 60g Parmesan, freshly grated
- 80g unsalted butter
- Salt and pepper

Risotto con Funghi Serves 4

Method

1. Put the stock in a pan, bring to the boil and keep at a low simmer.

2. Heat the olive oil or butter in a large pan over a low heat, add the onion and fry until soft, about 10 minutes. Add the button mushrooms and the porcini, and cook for 5 minutes, until soft and lightly browned.

3. Add the rice and stir for a minute or two, then add one or two ladles of boiling stock. Stir continuously over the heat, adding stock a ladleful at a time as each addition is absorbed. After 18-20 minutes, check for the required al dente texture – the rice should be tender, but with a firm bite in the centre, and the risotto should be moist .

4. Remove the pan from the heat, add the Parmesan and butter and stir in well. Season to taste, and serve on warm plates. Buon appetito.

Delia Smith

Brownies need introducing to those who have not yet made them. Yes, they are cakes but not in the conventional sense. They are supposed to be moist and squashy, and although they won't look as if they are cooked, they are. Don't think you may have failed, just bite into one and you'll never look back.

Ingredients

- 125g dark chocolate (minimum 70% cocoa solids), broken up
- 175g block butter
- 3 large eggs
- 275g golden caster sugar
- 75g plain flour
- 1 level teaspoon baking powder
- ¼ teaspoon salt
- 150g Brazil nuts, toasted and roughly chopped, or any other nuts, or a mixture.
- A Silverwood oblong tin 20cm by 26cm, 4 cm deep

Brazil Nut Brownie Method

Pre-heat the oven to 180°C, gas mark 4.

First put the broken-up chocolate and butter in a bowl over a pan containing 5cm of barely

simmering water, without the bowl touching the water. When it has melted (5–10 minutes) take it off the heat.

Next whisk the eggs and sugar lightly together – but don't overdo this. Stir the egg mixture and all the other ingredients into the chocolate.

Then pour the mixture into the tin and bake near the centre of the oven for 30 minutes until springy in the middle.

Leave the cake in the tin to go completely cold before dividing into roughly twelve squares and store in an airtight tin.

To watch a video how to make Delia's brownies go to the Delia Online Cookery School www.deliaonline.com

Paul Hollywood

The son of a baker, Paul originally trained as a sculptor before his father persuaded him to join the family business. He went on to become head baker at some of the most exclusive hotels, including Cliveden, The Chester Grosvenor and The Dorchester, gaining a reputation as an innovator and one of the country's finest artisan bakers. Following his apprenticeship and success at some of the UK's top hotels, Paul took the opportunity to travel extensively through Cyprus, Egypt and Jordan, visiting remote villages to discover ancient techniques for baking bread, and, on one occasion, travelling to a Bedouin encampment and baking in the dessert on an upturned cooking pot. Paul is currently judge on BBC 2's The Great British Bake Off.

Ingredients

- 500g strong white bread flour, plus a little more for dusting
- 10g salt
- 10g instant yeast
- 20g very soft, unsalted butter
- 300ml cool water
- Olive oil, for greasing

White Cob Bread Rolls

Makes: about 15 *Preparation Time:* 3 hours *Bake:* 20 minutes

Method

1. Tip the flour into a large mixing bowl and add the salt to one side of the bowl and the yeast to the other. Add the butter and three-quarters of the water and turn the mixture round with your fingers. Continue to add the remaining water, a little at a time, until you've picked up all of the flour from the sides of the bowl. You may not need to add all of the water, or you may need to add a little more - you want dough that is soft, but not soggy. Use the mixture to clean the inside of the bowl and keep going until the mixture forms a rough dough.

2. Tip the dough onto a lightly floured work surface and begin to knead. Keep kneading for 5-10 minutes. Work through the initial wet stage until the dough starts to form a soft, smooth skin. When your dough feels smooth and silky, put it into a lightly oiled bowl. Cover with a tea towel and leave to rise until at least doubled in size – this means at least one hour, but it's fine to leave it for two or even three hours.

3. Line two baking trays with baking parchment or silicone paper.

4. Tip the dough onto a lightly floured work surface. Without knocking the dough back first, use a rolling pin to roll it out into a rectangle about 2.5cm thick. Tack the dough to the work surface with your fingers along one of the longer edges - it's easier if you tack the edge closest to you. Roll up the dough back and towards you to form a long sausage, then lift the tacked bit into the sausage and roll the lot on the table to make sure that the dough sticks together. Cut the sausage into 3cm pieces and put them on the baking trays, flat side down. Put the trays inside clean plastic bags and leave to prove for at least half an hour, or until the dough is doubled in size and springs back quickly if you prod it lightly with your finger. Remove from plastic bags. Heat the oven to 220°C.

5. Bake for 15-20 minutes and enjoy warm.

Eric Lanlard

*E*ric Lanlard is an award winning master patissier and international baking star. He is author of five books – his latest 'Chocolat' is an exquisite collection of his stunning recipes, celebrating his favourite ingredient. Eric has presented four television series, Glamour Puds (series 1 and 2) and Baking Mad (series 1 and 2), and creates breathtaking cakes for numerous A List celebrities. His latest venture has been to design a themed series of Afternoon Teas, for the prestigious Jumeirah Carlton Tower Hotel in Knightsbridge, London. Eric's glamorous London HQ, Cake Boy, houses a thriving cookery school alongside a coffee and patissierie lounge and when he isn't flying across the globe for his prestigious clients and media commitments, there is nowhere that Eric would rather be.

RECIPE TAKEN FROM CHOCOLAT BY ERIC LANLARD PUBLISHED BY MITCHELL BEAZLEY © PHOTOGRAPHY, KATE WHITAKER

Ingredients

- 200g (7oz) dark chocolate, roughly chopped
- 150g (5oz) unsalted butter, plus extra for greasing
- 2 tsp vanilla paste or extract
- 150g (5oz) golden caster sugar
- 3 eggs, beaten
- 75g (3oz) plain flour
- 2 tbsp cocoa powder
- 1 tsp salt
- 100g (3½oz) dark chocolate chips

Devilish Choclate Brownies

Serves: 16 *Preparation Time:* 10 minutes

Cooking Time: 30 minutes

Method

1. Preheat the oven to 180°C (fan 160°C)/350°F/gas mark 4.

2. Grease a 19cm (7½in) square shallow baking tin andline the base with baking paper.

3. Melt the chopped chocolate, butter and vanilla together in a heatproof bowl set over a saucepan of barely simmering water, making sure the surface of the water does not touch the bowl. Remove from the heat and stir in the sugar, then leave to cool for a few minutes.

4. Beat in the eggs, then sift in the flour, cocoa and salt and fold in until the mixture is smooth and glossy. Stir in the chocolate chips.

5. Pour the mixture into the prepared tin and level the top. Bake in the oven for 25 minutes, or until the top starts to crack but the centre remains gooey. Turn off the oven and leave the brownies inside for a further 5 minutes before removing. Leave to cool completely in the tin.

6. Cut the brownies into 16 small squares and remove from the tin. Store in an airtight container for up to 4 days.

Gina Moffatt

A fun loving mother of two and a Princes' Trust backed-business woman. With a burning passion for flowers and food, Gina returns to her roots with this delicious Jerk Chicken offering.

Ingredients

- 8 Spring onions, chopped
- 4 large garlic cloves, chopped
- 3 Scotch bonnet chiles, chopped
- 1 small onion, chopped
- 1/4 cup sugar
- 2 tablespoons chopped thyme
- 2 tablespoons ground allspice
- Pinch of salt
- 1 1/4 teaspoons freshly grated nutmeg
- 1 teaspoon cinnamon
- 1/2 cup white vinegar
- 1/4 cup soy sauce
- 1/4 cup fresh lime juice
- 1/4 cup fresh orange juice
- 1/4 cup vegetable oil
- Three 4lb chickens, each cut into 8 pieces
- Freshly ground pepper
- Sweet Chilli Sauce
- Tomato sauce
- Water

Jerk Chicken
Method

1. Aim to marinate the chicken the night before you cook

2. In a food processor, combine all of the ingredients except the chicken and process to a paste. Put the chicken pieces in a very large bowl and pour the marinade on top. Toss to coat the chicken thoroughly. Cover and refrigerate overnight.

3. Light a grill. Remove the chicken pieces from the marinade, leaving on a coating of spice paste. Grill the chicken over moderately high heat, turning often, until the skin is nicely charred and the chicken is cooked through. Take out the chicken. Lastly, mix the sweet chilli sauce with tomato ketchup and water and add to keep the chicken moist. This all together should take about 30 minutes. Transfer to a platter and serve.

A beautiful former coaching inn dating back to 1767, in the heart of historic Wickham, *The King's Head* has truly made a name for itself with excellent quality home-cooked food, fine ales and a welcoming village vibe. The focus is on quality dishes, with daily seasonal specials. Sourced from hand-picked suppliers, many of whom are local to us. We cater for numerous celebrations and weddings too, in our delightfully quirky skittle alley, accommodating up to 130. We hope you enjoy our wonderful, homely pub and country dining.

Lymington Crab Avocado, Tomato, Lime Creme Fraiche, Cucumber and Pink Grapefruit Dressing

Method

1. Peel and segment the grapefruit neatly from the center of each segment, don't worry about getting the whole segment out as you want them to be fairly small and all the same size

2. With the remains of the grapefruit squeeze through a fine chinoix to remove all the juice.

3. Whisk together the mustard and vinegar slowly adding the grapefruit juice, then slowly whisk in the oil and lastly add the grenadine, this dressing is supposed to marble on the plate and is not a completely emulsified dressing so don't worry if it splits you can whisk it back together when you need it.

Method for dish

1. Bring a pot of water to the boil and add a tbsp. of salt

2. Remove vine from the tomatoes, remove the

Ingredients

White crab mix *(Mix all ingredients together and set aside)*
- 300g picked Limington white crab meat
- 30g mayo
- 60g finely diced red pepper
- ¼ bunch dill, picked and chopped, save half for the avocado
- 10g finely grated fresh horseradish
- Juice and zest of ½ lemon
- Salt and freshly ground black pepper

Brown Crab mix *(Mix all ingredients together and set aside)*
- 300g Picked Limington brown crab meat
- Juice of 1 lime
- ¼ bunch chives
- Salt and pepper to taste

Tomato Mix
- 4 plum tomatoes on the vine
- 1 banana shallot finely diced
- 1/8 bunch tarragon, picked down and roughly chopped
- 1tsp white wine vinegar
- 2 tsp extra virgin olive oil
- 1tsp Worcestershire sauce

Avocado Mix *(Mix all ingredients together and set aside)*
- 2 perfectly ripe avocados – peeled, core removed and finely diced
- Juice of one lemon
- Remaining chopped dill from above
- Salt to taste

Lime Crème Fraiche *– whip together with a whisk until light and fluffy*
- 200g crème fraiche
- Juice and zest of 1 lime
- 2 pinch salt
- 4 twists of fresh ground black pepper

Pink Grapefruit dressing
- 2 pink grapefruits
- 1tsp Dijon mustard
- 1tsp sherry vinegar
- 300ml olive oil
- 1tbsp grenadine

Garnish
- 1 cucumber, peeled, cut in half then deseeded and squared off evenly then diced into 1cm cubes
- Pink grapefruit segments
- Mixed Sakura cress, snipped and mixed together and lightly dressed with the pink grapefruit dressing

green core with a small knife and gently criss cross the top making sure not to go in too deep

3. Blanch each tomato in the boiling water for 8-10 seconds to crack the skin

4. Place the tomatoes straight into ice cold water to stop them from cooking and peel the skin, should come off easily, if not slightly longer in the water

5. Cut tomatoes into quarters, remove the seeds and dice the flesh finely

6. Mix with all the other ingredients and set aside

To Plate the Dish

1. 4 round glass plates, polished

2. In a ring approximately 6cm wide by 5cm tall start by neatly making the bottom layer with the Avocado mix above.

3. Keeping the layers even and leaving enough room for every layer now spoon in your brown crab mix followed by the white crab mix then the tomato layer and finally the crème fraiche

4. In the center of the plate neatly place the dressed cress about the size of the ring and then place the Tian on top of it.

5. Around the Tian, equal distances apart put 3 pink grapefruit segments and then in between them the cucumber cubes lightly dressed and seasoned and 3 of the Purple cress you have from your mixed Sakura cress.

6. Using a teaspoon drizzle the Pink grapefruit dressing around randomly some going over the cucumber and grapefruit segments.

London Porter Smoked Salmon Terrine, Cucumber, Quails Egg, Tomato Bread

A quintessential English country pub, set on the edge of one of the Country's most historic cricket grounds in Hambledon – dating back to 1750 and famous for developing the laws of modern day cricket. *The Bat and Ball* is not just famed for its cricketing history, but for a quality, freshly prepared menu specialising in local game, daily fish specials and seasonal British dishes. A traditional country affair, *The Bat and Ball* offers a wonderfully relaxed, traditional atmosphere and abundance of character, for year round dining.

Ingredients

- 400g London Porter Smoked Salmon
- 125g unsalted butter
- 125ml whipping cream
- Pink Peppercorns – crushed
- 1 Cucumber
- 12 Quale eggs
- Tomato Bread

Method

1. Clarify the butter, weigh out 150g smoked salmon and line the terrine mold.

2. Place the remaining salmon in blender and blend until smooth.

3. In separate pans warm the cream and clarified butter. Slowly add the cream and then the butter to the processed salmon and blend until smooth. Season with crushed pink peppercorns

4. Transfer salmon mixture to terrine mold, cover with Clingfilm and set overnight

5. Bring a pan of salted water to the boil and carefully put your eggs in the pan for two minutes, then place in to iced water. Once they have chilled peel and set aside

6. Peel your cucumber in to long strips and roll you will need two cucumber rolls per plate

7. Slice your terrine and arrange one slice on to your plate, cut your quails egg in half, add one egg and the cucumber rolls to each plate. Slice the tomato bread and add two slices on each plate

Ingredients

- 2kg butternut squash
- 6 small onions - peeled and chopped
- 4 large garlic cloves – peeled and crushed
- 2 tablespoons of olive oil
- 2 litres vegetable stock
- 25g butter
- Salt and pepper

Meridians Marvellous Butternut Squash Soup

Serves: 10

Method

1. Pre-heat the oven to 220°C.

2. Peel, deseed and chop the butternut squash into 1 inch cubes.

3. Cover the cubes in a thin layer of oil (using 1 of the 2 tablespoons) and throw into a roasting tin.

4. Roast the squash for 30-40 mins until the squashes soften but be careful to ensure they don't burn.

5. Whilst the squash is roasting, chop onions into small chunks, peel and crush the garlic.

6. Fry onions and garlic in butter and remaining oil on a low heat until the onions are soft but not browned (around 20 minutes).

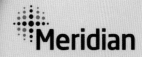

7. Heat the vegetable stock in a large pan and add the squashes, onions and garlic into the pan to simmer.

8. Finally pour contents of the pan into a blender and blend to desired thickness.

9. Season with salt and pepper to serve.

10. Enjoy with a hearty wedge of warm crusty bread and melted butter (not included in the calorie count!)

*E*stablished in 2002, *Meridian* is the largest independent corporate finance boutique on the South Coast.

Meridian works with clients to help them determine their strategic aims and to assist them in bringing about a change of shareholding or fundraising. This includes marketing businesses for sale and project managing, mergers and acquisitions, management buy-outs/ buy-ins and raising bank or equity finance.

Meridian also provides ongoing strategic advice to companies through retained appointments and non-executive roles as well as valuation advice for shareholders wishing to understand the value of their businesses.

Meridian has an enviable record of successful transactions – completing over 90% of engagements, which is well above the industry average. The Meridian team encompasses a broad skill set relevant to deal making and members of our team have worked directly in industry, accountancy, banking, venture capital, due diligence and corporate law.

Ham Hock And Parsley Terrine With Ravigote Sauce

Serves: 8 *Preparation time:* 25 minutes
Cooking time: 3 hours + overnight refrigeration

Ingredients

For the terrine:

- 2 ham hocks (about 1 kg each)
- 2 carrots
- 2 celery sticks
- 1 onion
- 10 peppercorns
- 1 bunch of fresh parsley
- 100g baby gherkins sliced
- 2 gelatine leaves

For the ravigote sauce:

- 2tbsp chopped capers
- 1tsp chopped parsley
- 1tsp chopped chervil
- 1tsp chopped tarragon
- 1tsp Dijon mustard
- 1tbsp chopped shallots
- 1 hard boiled egg chopped
- 2tbsp sherry vinegar
- 5tbsp extra virgin rapeseed oil
- 3tbsp ham hock cooking stock
- Salt and pepper to taste

Method

1. Put the ham in a large saucepan, with the halved carrots, celery sticks, halved onion and peppercorns. Cover with cold water and bring to the boil.

2. Reduce the heat, cover and simmer for 3 hours until very tender.

3. Remove the ham from the pan and set aside. Allow the stock to cool down.

4. Meanwhile, line a terrine mould with cling film.

5. Once the ham is cold, tear the meat off the bone into strips and discard as much fat and skin as you can. Put into a large bowl and add the chopped parsley and sliced gherkins. Mix together and spoon into the lined terrine mould.

6. Soak the gelatine in plenty of cold water for about 5 minutes. Measure 300ml cooking stock and put into a separate saucepan and warm through Take the gelatine out of the water and squeeze out the excess water. Drop into the warm cooking stock and stir until melted.

7. Carefully pour the stock over the ham into the terrine mould and cover the top with cling film to seal in the terrine.

8. Put in the fridge to set overnight. The terrine will keep for up to 6 days in the fridge.

9. For the ravigote, whisk vinegar, stock and mustard in a medium bowl to blend. Gradually whisk in oil. Stir in tarragon, parsley, capers, shallots, gherkins and the hardboiled egg.

FOUR SEASONS HOTEL
Hampshire

*S*et within a 500 acre historical estate, *Four Seasons Hotel Hampshire* combines luxury with local in order to provide a memorable dining experience.

Our two main restaurants are both strongly influenced by the wealth of ingredients produced in our wonderful county and menus change frequently in order to reflect the season.

'Seasons' offers a French-European inspired menu, showcasing locally sourced seafood on FiSH Fridays and offers a twist on a traditional roast in the form of the Farmer's Market Lunch every Sunday. 'The Bistro' offers contemporary home-style favourites with home smoked produce.

Traditional Afternoon Tea can be enjoyed in The Library Lounge whilst Asian inspired dishes are served alongside The Spa in Café Santé.

43

Cheese and Watercress Scones

Serves: 12 *Preparation time:* 25 minutes
Cooking time: 15 Minutes

Method

1. Sift the flour and salt together and rub in the butter.

2. Stir in the cheese and chopped watercress and bind with water to make a soft dough.

3. Roll out on a floured board until about 1 inch thick.

4. Cut into 2 inch circles using a pastry cutter.

5. Bake at 200°C, gas mark 6 until risen and browned (about 15 minutes).

6. Delicious simply with butter, or as part of a ploughman's lunch.

Ingredients

- 100g/4oz self-raising wholemeal flour
- 100g/4oz butter, cubed
- 100g/4oz self-raising plain flour
- ½ tsp salt
- 50g/2oz Gruyère cheese, grated
- 1 x 85g/3oz pack watercress, chopped

VITACRESS

El Sabio

TAPAS BAR &
RESTAURANT

Tortilla Espanola

Method

1. Slice the onion thinly and put it on the hob in a skillet along with the olive oil. Turn the hob on a medium heat and simmer it. Meanwhile, slice your potatoes again thinly and also put that in the pan. Season with some sea salt and fry them together until the potato slices are soft.

2. Once the potatoes and the onion are soft, use a sieve and drain them. Do not throw the oil away.

3. Combine this with the eggs and season it with some black pepper and sea salt.

4. Put your skillet back on the hob, heat the saved oil in it and wait until it's hot enough, using high heat.

5. Your oil should smoke a little bit, pour the above mixture into the pan but be careful with the oil, as it will be very hot.

6. Stir a little until the mixture gets thick, turn the heat down and leave it until the bottom gets light brown. Move your pan a little to prevent it sticking to the bottom.

7. Finally, use a ceramic plate to turn it on the other side and place it back into the pan and cook it until the other side also gets light brown.

Ingredients

- 1 quarter of a large Spanish onion.
- 2 medium sized potatoes
- 2 large eggs
- Sea salt
- Ground black pepper
- 100ml Olive oil

PARSONAGE

Pork, Leek and Ginger Lollies

Serves: 4 as a starter (or 2 as a main dish)

Method

1. Mix all the ingredients together in a bowl.

2. Divide into 12 and squash into small balls.

3. Thread 3 balls onto a stick with a slice of salami between each.

4. Wrap the end of the stick in tinfoil.

4. Cook under the grill or in the oven 10 - 15 minutes.

5. Serve on a bed of salad with a sweet chilli dipping sauce.

6. Peppers or mushrooms could be threaded between the pork balls to make a main course.

Ingredients

- 440g pork shoulder - minced (good quality, traditional breed)

- 80g leek - finely chopped

- 1 cm root ginger finely grated

- 8 slices of salami (British is best!)

- Salt and pepper

- Wooden stick/skewer

HAMPSHIRE · CHARCUTERIE

Ingredients

- 2 slices Boudin Noir per skewer

- 2 slices chorizo per skewer

- 1 red onion roughly cut to size of meat

- 1 red pepper roughly cut to size of meat

Boudin Noir Kebabs

Method

1. Griddle the 'red' ingredients.

2. Cool and place on a skewer alternating with slices of Boudin Noir.

3. Brush lightly with olive oil and re-heat on the barbecue.

Ingredients

- 600g fresh salmon
- 4 small trout fillets (small diced)
- 2 egg whites
- 400ml double cream
- 2tsp chives finely chopped
- Salt and pepper, to taste

Smoked Trout Sausages

Method

1. Puree the fresh salmon and add egg white until well combined.
2. Gradually pulse half the cream into the mix. Transfer the mix to a large mixing bowl.
3. Fold in the diced smoked trout. Cover and put in the fridge for 30 minutes.

BH
Brookfield Hotel

The Hermitage Restaurant has been integral to The Brookfield Hotel's success for many years.

Seating up to 120 people for a formal banquet, it is also a delightful venue for more relaxed occasions, such as family celebrations and business successes.

The spacious restaurant, overlooking the gardens, offers a regularly changing Table d'hote menu, while snacks and bar meals are available from the bar and adjoining lounge.

Sunday lunch is popular with local residents and visitors alike; our 2-course weekday lunch is so popular it has to be booked in advance, to be certain of obtaining a table.

Wine tasting dinners, fish suppers and themed evenings are all held regularly.

Working breakfasts, morning coffee, lunch, afternoon tea and dinner are all well catered for by The Brookfield kitchens, presided over by our popular head chef, whilst our restaurant and bar manager is always happy to recommend a suitable wine to enhance your dining experience.

4 Remove from fridge and fold in the rest of the cream.

5 Add the chives plus salt and pepper. Place back in the fridge for 10 mins.

6. Remove from fridge and place mixture into a piping bag.

7. Pipe onto cling film around 4/5 inches long and roll into sausage shapes and tie each end.

8. Place rolls in a hot water bath for 4/5 minutes, then chill as quickly as possible.

Hampshire Wine School

Mulled Wine

Serves: 4

Method

1. In a saucepan, pour half the wine, along with the clementine juice, clementine peel, orange slices, lemon peel, sugar, bayleaf and all the spices. Heat gently until the sugar has dissolved, stirring occasionally. Taste to see if you want the wine sweeter, and add more sugar to taste. Bring to the boil and reduce for 15 minutes until you have a thick syrup. Strain. You can freeze this syrup into ice cube trays and use at a later stage (saving you a lot of time on Christmas day!). Otherwise, pour your hot syrup back into your saucepan and carry on with the second part of the recipe.

2. Add the rest of the wine into the infused syrup. Let it simmer very gently, stirring regularly, for about 10 minutes (do not let it boil though, since we do not want to burn off the rest of the alcohol!), and enjoy the fabulously fragrant aromas of the sweet spices and let them warm you up and fill the kitchen.

3. Off the heat, stir in the Grand Marnier if you are using it.

4. Pour into heatproof glasses and serve at once.

Ingredients

- 1 bottle of red wine
- 60g / 2oz white caster sugar
- 60ml / 2floz clementine juice
- 1 cinnamon stick
- 5 cloves
- 5cm/2in piece fresh root ginger, peeled and sliced
- 1 pinch of freshly grated nutmeg
- 1 orange, sliced
- 1 lemon, peel only
- 1 clementine, peel only
- 1 dried bay leaf
- 60ml / 2floz Grand Marnier (optional, but rather nice)

Ingredients

- 1 pork fillet trimmed
- 3 large potatoes peeled
- 3 Granny smith apples peeled
- 500g parsnips
- 250g baby carrot
- 1 medium onion peeled and finely sliced
- 6 Crab apples
- 500ml stock syrup
- 500ml fresh chicken stock
- 250g girolle mushrooms cleaned
- 100ml double cream
- 100g butter
- 25ml vanilla essence
- 100ml apple juice
- 50g Demerara sugar
- Micro salad leaves
- Gravy

Romsey Pork Fillet, Braised Potato, Parsnip Puree, Crab Apple and Girolles

Method

1. Take the potatoes and slice thinly (use a mandolin if available) and layer in a lined casserole dish to cover the bottom. Scatter the sliced onion over the potato and season. Repeat this till you have 4 or 5 layers of potato. Pour over 200ml of the chicken stock cover with foil and bake in the oven at 175°c for 25 minutes or until a knife goes through the potatoes unassisted. If possible chill overnight.

2. Remove the core from the apples and chop into small even sized pieces put in a small saucepan with the vanilla, sugar

A historic, incredibly charming pub with rooms in the heart of Winchester, *The Wykeham Arms* is nestled between the Cathedral and the 14th century college. Steeped in heritage, we offer high quality dining with locally-sourced ingredients, coupled with a menu of 70 hand-picked wines and 5 real ales, in our very charming surroundings. A unique Pub, in a beautiful spot.

and apple juice and cook on a low heat until the apples are breaking up. Transfer to a food processor and pulse to a smooth consistency.

3. Peel the parsnip and remove the woody centre and chop in small even pieces, along with the remaining chicken stock put in a pan and cover and cook on a moderate heat until the parsnip are breaking up. Place into a food processor add the cream and pulse till smooth. Season to taste

4. Wash the crab apples and place in a pan with the stock syrup cover and gently simmer. You want to be able to push a knife through with a little effort.

5. In a hot pan seal the seasoned pork and put on a baking tray and finish in the oven 175°c 18 minutes, the pork should be firm to touch. Put a plate somewhere warm to rest before carving.

6. Remove the potato from the casserole dish and cut into rectangles of 2x3inches ,place on baking paper and cook in the oven (175°c) for 15 minutes

7. Cover the baby carrots with cold water bring to the boil and simmer until tender.

8. In a hot pan melt the butter and cook the girolles until soft and drain on kitchen paper.

9. To build the dish take a dessert spoon and swipe the parsnip puree to one side of the plate. Carefully place half the girolles and baby carrots on top of the potato, slice the pork about 5 slices a portion and place on the parsnip puree, dot the apple puree randomly about the plate (4 or 5 dots) and scatter the remaining. Place the micro salad leaves on top of the pork and drizzle the gravy around the plate.

Glazed Ham Hock, 3 Hour Duck Egg, Vanilla Glazed Pineapple and Watercress

Serves: 4

Ingredients

- 2x ham hocks
- 4x duck eggs
- 1x onion
- 2x carrots
- 1x garlic clove
- 2 x bay leaves
- Peppercorns
- Pineapple
- 200ml stock syrup
- 6x large Maris Pipers
- Honey
- Thyme
- Olive oil
- Watercress for garnish
- Vanilla Pods

Method

Hocks

1. Remove hocks from the packs they arrive in and place in a pot, leave under a tap with cold running water for ten minutes to refresh, clean and remove some of the salt content.

2. Roughly chop onions, carrots, garlic, add bay leaves and peppercorns and cook the hocks slowly, topping up the water as necessary until the hocks are tender so that the meat can easily be removed from the bone.

3. Gently pull the meat off in chunks and allow to cool.

4. Pass the stock

5. Portion the hock into vacuum packs adding a little bit of the stock to each pouch.

Pineapple

1. Peel the pineapple with a knife and then quarter it. Remove the core, square off and cut into equally sized perfect cubes.

2. Make stock syrup of equal amounts of water and sugar and scrape in vanilla pods.

3. Put 3 cubes of pineapple in a vacuum bag with a small ladle of vanilla syrup and seal

At *The Links Tavern* we're a delightfully restored pub & dining room, offering sophisticated yet uncomplicated Hampshire dining. Our Head Chef Adam and his talented team offer a regularly changing menu of seasonal produce and pub classics, plus the option of booking our Chef's Table for an evening of fine food and wines, tailored to you. For a more relaxed affair in our main bar, children, dogs, and muddy boots are always welcome.

Egg

. Cook in the water bath on 62°C for 3 hours then chill.

. Watercress must be picked down really well and not bruised, lightly dressed last minute.

Chips

Must be peeled, perfectly squared off, and triple cooked as follows.

Wash well with cold water, bring up to a simmer then drain on cloth but do not wash off, allow to steam dry themselves.

Blanch in fryer on 130°C to seal and almost cook through.

4. Drain off then place on trays with parchment paper and dry out in oven on 160°C (no moisture to dry out.)

5. Refrigerate then cook 180°C until crispy.

To Service

1. Water bath the hock and egg until it's away then ham hock goes into a hot pan with honey, thyme and oil to crisp up pineapple also into a little pan and slightly caramelize in its stock syrup.

2. Crack egg as you would a normal egg and place on the plate next to the hock.

3. Stack on chips and a bit of watercress.

Twice Cooked Pork Belly, Red Onion Marmalade, Salt Baked Turnip, Apple Pearls

Ingredients

For the pork

- ½ a whole pork belly, about 1½ kg from a rare breed if possible (like Gloucester Old Spot, Tamworth Etc) boned, skin left on but not scored
- 2 star anise
- 2 tsp coriander seeds
- 1 tbsp sea salt
- Handful thyme
- Handful rosemary
- 2 x 350g jars goose or duck fat
- 6 curly parsley sprigs

Red onion marmalade

- 250g red onion sliced
- 1 garlic clove finely chopped
- 200ml red wine
- 100ml Madeira
- 60g sugar
- 10 leaves of Gelatin

Salt baked Swede

- 1xSwede
- 600g salt
- 120g egg white
- 120g flour
- 50g butter

Apple Pearls

- 50g apple juice
- 1Tsp lemon juice
- 25g sugar
- 25g water 1
- 0.5g Agar
- 1lt vegetable oil

Method

Pork

1. With a pestle and mortar, crush the coriander seeds with the star anise, then stir through the salt. Season the pork on both sides with the salt mix. Place the pork, skin side up, in an ovenproof dish that is just large enough to hold it. Scatter over the herbs, cling film the whole thing, then leave overnight in the fridge

2. Heat oven to 150°C/fan 130°C/gas 2. Empty the goose fat into a saucepan and heat until liquid and starting to simmer.

3. Ladle the fat over the pork; add sunflower oil to cover if you need to. Cover the dish with foil, then cook the pork in the oven, undisturbed, for 3 hours by which time it will be very tender.

4. Remove the dish from the oven and leave it to settle for 10 minutes. Meanwhile, line a tray with a piece of greaseproof paper. Carefully lift the pork from the fat and pick off any herbs. Lay it on the paper, skin side down.Cut another piece of paper and lay it over the pork. Cover with a tray, weighed down to press and leave in fridge overnight to set.

Marmalades

1. Sweat the onion and garlic down slowly for 25 minutes until very soft

2. Add the sugar cook for 5mins Add the liquor and cook slowly until all the liquor has reduced so it is sticky

3. Weigh the mix and allocates 2 leaves of gelatin to 100g of mix Mix the soaked gelatin leaves into the hot marmalade mix strain dry in a conical strainer

4. Then roll thin between greaseproof paper and freeze, and then cut from frozen 15cmx5cm strips

5. Refreeze and peel off the paper before serving on a hot plate

Swede

1. Mix the egg whites and salt together then mix the flour to create a sticky dough

2. Moisten the outside of the Swede then coat the entire Swede with the salt crust Cook at 180°C oven for 2 hours leave to cool

3. Crack open the and remove the skin crush into a pan adding butter and seasoning to taste

LAINSTON HOUSE HOTEL

*Just a couple of miles outside of Winchester, the stunning 17th century five star *Lainston House Hotel* is one of the best kept culinary secrets in Hampshire. The gorgeous views down the mile-long avenue of lime trees and the Avenue Restaurant (3 AA Rosettes) are perfect reasons to visit this most elegant venue for a spot of lunch, afternoon tea, dinner, a birthday celebration in one of their private rooms or just a cupper with a friend. Dine alfresco in the summer sunshine or get all cosy in luxuriously deep sofas next to a roaring log fire in the colder months. Provenance, seasonality and local produce are the key focus for our kitchen brigade. The chefs' passion and influences stem from the vibrant kitchen garden which provides the majority of the vegetables and fruit to the hotel's kitchen. You are guaranteed the finest, freshest produce in everything you eat!Look out for the enticing open air and foodie events that take place throughout the year!

Apple Pearls

1. Place a tray of vegetable oil in the freezer to get ice cold Boil the entire ingredients together and then cool. Place mix into a 'squirty' bottle and squirt into the cold oil. Drain the pearls from the oil wash the pearls well Store in the fridge until required

2. When you are ready to cook the pork, heat oven to 220°C/ fan 200°C/ gas 7. Remove pork from the tray, and then peel away paper. Lightly score the skin with a sharp knife and trim the edges, so you can then cut out 6-8 rectangles portions sizes

3. To cook the pork, heat a drizzle of oil in a large non-stick ovenproof pan. Lay the pork, skin side down, and leave for a few mins to crackle, then place the pan in the oven and cook for 20 minutes. Remove from the oven and check to see that the skin has blistered, then carefully flip it over and cook the underside for 3 minutes just to heatthrough

4. Present the dish with onion marmalade placed on to a hot plate a quenelle of the crushed salt baked Swede, apple pearls and the crispy belly pork •Serving suggestion serve with your best rich Madeira sauce recipe and a little apple puree.

Ingredients

- 220 g belly pork
- 5 asparagus spears, blanched
- 100g new potatoes/ Jersey Royals, quartered, sautéed
- 75g Hampshire black pudding, pan fried
- 50 ml wholegrain mustard sauce

Pork Belly, Black Pudding and Asparagus

Method

For the belly pork:

1. Pre heat the fan oven to 200°C.
2. Pat the skin of the pork belly dry and score.
3. Rub in salt & pepper and roast for 30 minutes.
4. Reduce heat to 110°C and roast for further 3 hours or until tender.

5. If necessary place under the salamander grill to crisp up the crackling.

6. Leave to rest for 10 minutes.

For the wholegrain mustard sauce:

1. Sautee 150 g finely chopped shallots for 10 minutes, without colouring.

2. Add 150 ml white wine and reduce by half.

3. Add 300 ml double cream; bring to the boil and strain.

4. Stir in 1 TBSP wholegrain mustard and season.

O wtons Farm Shops, traditional butchers have traded in the Southampton area for 35 years and have now expanded to over the last three years. With three shops and a fourth opening in March 2014, Owtons are succeeding where other independent butchers are failing. The three stores are located at Chalcroft farm West End Southampton, Kimbridge Farm Shop Nr Romsey, Garsons Garden Centre Titchfield and Country Market Bordon opens 2014. With quality local produce at the forefront we aim to bring you the best of what Hampshire can provide.

We work with 25 local farmers providing us with the best Pork, Lamb and Beef from around the area, including Beef from our very own farm in West End, Southampton, which is hung for 3 weeks. Our Knowledgeable onsite butcher is able to provide you provenance and advice on which cut to choose with cooking advice where necessary.

Mackerel Salad with Oyster Mayonnaise

Serves: 6
Cooking time: 2mins
Preparation time: 30mins

Ingredients

* ✳ 6 Fresh Mackerel Fillets
* ✳ 1 Baby Gem
* ✳ 6 Oysters
* ✳ 1 Lemon
* ✳ Black Pepper
* ✳ Vegetable Oil 240g
* ✳ Olive Oil 140g

Method

1. Start by making the mayonnaise.
2. Open the oysters, put the juice in another dish, place the oysters in ice water and gently wash off all debris and any cracked shell. Place oysters and the juices in a blender, blitz and slowly add both the Olive Oil and Vegetable Oil, then season with a good squeeze of lemon juice and cracked black pepper.

*L*ime Wood is set in the heart of the New Forest, just outside the small town of Lyndhurst, we like to think of ourselves as a luxury country house hotel with a difference. Food is by Hartnett Holder & Co a relaxed, stylish and comfortable upscale restaurant - full of character, yet unpretentious. Angela Hartnett and Head Chef Luke Holder, with their team, create locally sourced English dishes with a respectful nod to the seasons and to Italian culinary ideologies. This collaboration is reflected in their fresh, confident approach ensuring that this is "fun dining, not fine dining". Hartnett and Holder's food is out-and-out British yet comes with the much loved Italian approach to eating - where sharing and provenance is everything.

Then you need to cure the mackerel fillets.
To make the cure use the grated zest of 1 lemon, 30g salt and 30g sugar and place over the fillets for 6 minutes, then wash off.

To assemble:

5. Cut the baby gem into quarters and season them before grilling them until they're slightly wilted (approx 1 min). Grill the mackerel very slightly (approx 1 - 2 mins) and serve pink.

6. Spoon a large dollop of the oyster mayonnaise on the plate, add the warmed baby gem and grilled mackerel and garnish with wild cresses.

Spaghetti with Isle of Wight Lobster

Ingredients

* 1Lb Lobster
* 200 G Fresh Spaghetti
* 1 Tin Chopped Tomatoes
* 1 Bulb Garlic
* 1 Large Onion
* 1 Tsp Olive Oil
* 1 Tsp Tomato Puree
* Salt & Pepper
* Lobster Oil
* Fresh Chilli
* Fresh Parsley
* Fresh Herbs

For The Tomato Sauce:

* 1 Whole Bulb Of Garlic
* 1 Tin Chopped Tomato
* 1 Large Onion
* 1 Tsp Olive Oil
* Seasoning

Serves: 6
Cooking time: 2mins
Preparation time: 30mins

Method

1. Roast the lobster shells for 20minutes in the oven at 160C with 1 tsp of tomato puree and 2tbs olive oil. Leave to stand for 24 hours.

2. Cook down the garlic and onions in a little olive oil add the tin tomato and reduce slowly till deep rich in red colour and the sauce is nice and thick.

3. Blanch lobster tail for 4 minutes. Blanch claws for 6 minutes add to ice water. Once cool shred the meat keeping it as chunky as possible.

4. Blanch the pasta, add tomato sauce, fresh chilli, shaved garlic, oil, herbs and finish with 2 tbs of lobster oil and a good sprinkle of parsley.

LIMEWOOD

Lime Wood is set in the heart of the New Forest, just outside the small town of Lyndhurst, we like to think of ourselves as a luxury country house hotel with a difference. Food is by Hartnett Holder & Co a relaxed, stylish and comfortable upscale restaurant - full of character, yet unpretentious. Angela Hartnett and Head Chef Luke Holder, with their team, create locally sourced English dishes with a respectful nod to the seasons and to Italian culinary ideologies. This collaboration is reflected in their fresh, confident approach ensuring that this is "fun dining, not fine dining". Hartnett and Holder's food is out-and-out British yet comes with the much loved Italian approach to eating - where sharing and provenance is everything.

Ingredients

- 24 oz of Raw Boneless Leg of lamb (3/4" Dice)
- 1 Cup of Olive Oil
- 12 oz Goat's Cheese.
- I Tbl Spoon Jerk Seasoning
- 24 Slices of Cooked Red Potatoes
- 4 Tomatoes (Small dice)
- Cucumber (small dice)
- Carrot Grated
- Tbl Of Balsamic Vinaigrette
- 2 Little Gem Lettuce (rough chop)
- Marinate lamb with oil and seasoning 24 Hours ahead

Grilled Spicy Lamb Salad

Serves: 4

Method

1. Place Goat's cheese on each potato and store on large plate. Place Iamb in frying pan at a medium heat, turning regularly. Whilst lamb is cooking, toss salad, tomatoes and cucumber with balsamic vinaigrette and serve into 4 chilled salad bowls.

2. Place goat's cheese topped potatoes under grill to warm up and turn light brown.

3. Once lamb is cooked to medium rare place on top of salads, surround the meat with the potato rounds and sprinkle salad with grated carrot.

The Hermitage Restaurant has been integral to The Brookfield Hotel's success for many years.

Seating up to 120 people for a formal banquet, it is also a delightful venue for more relaxed occasions, such as family celebrations and business successes.

The spacious restaurant, overlooking the gardens, offers a regularly changing Table d'hote menu, while snacks and bar meals are available from the bar and adjoining lounge.

Sunday lunch is popular with local residents and visitors alike; our 2-course weekday lunch is so popular it has to be booked in advance, to be certain of obtaining a table.

Wine tasting dinners, fish suppers and themed evenings are all held regularly.

Working breakfasts, morning coffee, lunch, afternoon tea and dinner are all well catered for by The Brookfield kitchens, presided over by our popular head chef, whilst our restaurant and bar manager is always happy to recommend a suitable wine to enhance your dining experience.

Trio of Greenfield Pork with Textures of Apple

Serves: 4

Ingredients

- 1/2 Greenfield Pork belly
- 8 x Greenfield Pork cheeks
- 4 carrots
- 1 celery
- 2 white onions
- 1 cinnamon stick
- 6 bay leaves
- 2 star anise
- 10 pepper corns
- 3 tbs olive oil
- 3 litres boiling chicken stock.

Method

1. Roughly Dice your carrots,celery and onion into a ince dice.

2. In a heavy bottom pan add the olive oil and heat until there's a slight haze, add peppercorns,cinimon,star anise and bayleaf cooking until slightly brown.

3. Now add the vegetables and leave to colour nicely for around 10/15 minutes. Once coloured heavily add the boiling chicken stock and bring to the boil.

4. Once boiling reduce to a simmer and add your belly and cheeks.

5. Now allow to cook for 3/4 hours on a very low simmer making sure the belly is fully submerged.

6. Once cooked the belly will be very soft to touch and the cheeks also remove them from the stock onto a large tray allow to cool,then refrigerate.

7. The stock can now be passed throw a sieve and placed into a clean pan, now reduce by three quarters and use as gravy/ jus.

8. Once the cheeks are cold trim the fat off ready to place into your gravy before serving to serve.

9. The belly can now have the skin and fat removed from the top leave a little fat so it can crisp later, on the under side remove ribs and discard, now portion into eight nice cubes.

10. Place in fridge ready to fry to serve later.

*T*he Blue Bell Inn Emsworth *Public House* offers a comfortable space in which to meet friends and socialise and is well stocked with a wide range of Real ales some of which are local, lagers, wines and spirits.

The Blue Bell has developed a reputation for delivering fine food at reasonable prices under the watchful eye of owner Giles and head chef Steve. See what the fuss is about.

Only yards from the harbour quay,this busy local is at the heart of the community, its the perfect spot for a drink or a bite to eat after a walk around the harbour.

We pride ourself on the quality of the food at The Blue Bell, with it all being made in house, and using local suppliers were ever possible which helps support the local economy.

Pork Fillet In Pancheeta

Ingredients

- 1 Greenfield Pork fillet
- 4 slices of pancheeta

Method

Trim all sinew and fat from the pork fillet once trimmed wrap the pancheeta around the fillet and roll in cling-film and refrigerate

Recipe continued on next page...

Spiced Apple Puree

Method

1. Peel and dice the green apples making sure to remove the core,

2. In a sauce pan melt the butter until golden brown then add the apples, thyme, cinnamon, star anise and sea salt cook until soft then add the sugar and water, allow the water to evaporate and apples to start to break down now remove from heat and purée either in a food processor or with a hand blender.

3. Leave to one side cover ready to serve.

Ingredients

- 3 x green apples
- 2 x sprigs of thyme
- 1/2 tsp ground cinnamon
- 1 x star anise
- 75g unsalted butter
- 2 tsp castor sugar
- 2 tsp water
- 1 pinch sea salt

Apple and Celeriac Remoularde

Method

1. Grate the apple and celeriac on a fine grater.

2. In a mixing bowl add the yolk, lemon juice, vinegar and mustard whisk until smooth now slowly very slowly add the oil allowing to thicken and emulsify. Once thick season and mix in parsley.

3. With the apple and celeriac mix the mayonnaise mixture through until just slightly coated.

4. Leave ready to serve

Ingredients

- 1x green apple
- 1/4 celeriac
- 1 x egg yolk
- 1/2 lemon juiced
- 1 tsp white wine vinegar
- 6 tsp vegetable oil
- 1/2 tsp Dijon mustard
- Seasoning
- Chopped parsley

There is little doubt that Emsworth is a unique place, positioned at the top of Chichester Harbour. This pretty, old fishing town would be just as happy sitting by the sea in Cornwall or even Brittany. In the main, the fishing boats and its once famous oyster industry may have gone, but Emsworth, unlike so many similar communities has still managed to maintain its sense of place.

Part of the reason for this is the fact that Emsworth still has a wonderful array of independent shops, pubs and restaurants. There are very few small towns left on the south coast that can still offer two family owned butchers, a greengrocers and a fishmongers. Add into the mix some of the area's finest restaurants and some wonderful traditional pubs and you can see why Emsworth is cherished both by its residents and visitors alike.

THE
BLUE BELL
INN

Ingredients

- 2 green apples
- 3 tbs self raising flour
- 6 tbs sparkling water
- Seasoning

Apple Fritter

The Blue Bell Inn Emsworth Public House offers a comfortable space in which to meet friends and socialise and is well stocked with a wide range of Real ales some of which are local, lagers, wines and spirits.

The Blue Bell has developed a reputation for delivering fine food at reasonable prices under the watchful eye of owner Giles and head chef Steve. See what the fuss is about.

Only yards from the harbour quay,this busy local is at the heart of the community, its the perfect spot for a drink or a bite to eat after a walk around the harbour.

We pride ourself on the quality of the food at The Blue Bell, with it all being made in house, and using local suppliers were ever possible which helps support the local economy.

Method

1. Peel the apples and core, try to keep neat and tidy, cut into rings around half a inch thick.

2. Mix the flour water and seasoning together until you have a thick batter.

To Finish The Dish

1 First sear the pork fillet in a pan and colour all sides once coloured remove onto a tray and drizzle with honey, wipe out the pan and repeat with the method with your cubes of pork belly.

2. Now place in a oven at 170°C for 15 minutes.

3. Place your cheeks and gravy/jus on the stove and allow to boil reduce until the gravy coats the cheeks and there glossy.

4. In a pan warm some oil around 1/4 inch until hot, then dip your apple rings in flour then batter and fry until golden brown.

5. Once brown remove and drain on kitchen towel.

Now Serve

1. Warm your apple purée in a pan and spread on 4 warm plate, place the apple fritter in middle, now slice the fillet into sixteen nice slices and lay 4 per plate next to it.

2. Place 2 cubes of belly per plate next to the fillet and top with a spoon of apple and celeriac remoularde.

3. Now place 2 cheeks on each plate and add gravy/jus to finish.

Marwell Venison, Braised Red Cabbage, Parsnip Puree, Goats Cheese Gnocchi *Serves* 4

Ingredients

Venison

- 600g Loin of venison fillet
- Sea salt and cracked black pepper
- A little oil (I use sunflower) and a few cold cubes of butter for cooking

Braised red cabbage

- 1 small red cabbage
- 100g butter
- 150g light brown sugar
- 75ml sherry vinegar or red wine vinegar

Parsnip puree

- 2 parsnips
- 150ml milk
- 75ml double cream
- 25g butter

Goats cheese gnocchi

- 500ml Milk
- 150g semolina
- 50g freshly grated parmesan cheese
- 1 large free range egg
- Fresh goats cheese
- Nutmeg
- A little oil for greasing
- Sea salt and freshly cracked black pepper

Method

Goats cheese gnocchi
Preparation Time 30 minutes,

Cooking Time 25 minutes.

Preheat an oven to 180 degrees Celsius. Pour the milk into a saucepan and season with salt, pepper and freshly grated nutmeg. Mix in the semolina and bring to a simmer over a gentle heat, stirring continuously. The mixture will thicken into a dough. Stir in the freshly grated parmesan and lightly beaten egg. Season with salt and pepper. Pour half of the mixture into an oiled baking tray, slice the goats cheese and lay it on top. Pour over the remaining mix. Cover the gnocchi with buttered greaseproof paper and place the tray into a larger baking tray half filled with hot water and bake in the oven. Do not let any of the water get into the gnocchi mixture. Cook until firm to touch (about 25 minutes) then remove from the oven. Discard the larger baking tray and water. Leave gnocchi to cool to room temperature then refrigerate. Once fully chilled cut into your desired shape.

Braised red cabbage
Preparation Time 10 minutes

Cooking Time 1 hour 30 minutes

Preheat an oven to 200 degrees C. Half, core and finely shred the cabbage. Melt the butter with sugar and vinegar in a pan over a low heat. When the sugar has dissolved, tip in the cabbage and toss to evenly coat. Cover with greaseproof paper and cook on a low heat for 1 hour 30 minutes so the cabbage is tender (Keep checking and stirring the cabbage every now and then). If there is still a fair amount of liquid remaining, remove the cabbage with a slotted spoon and put to one side. Reduce the liquid over a high heat to a syrup sauce. Then pour over the cabbage and toss to coat. Add salt and pepper to your taste.

Parsnip puree
Preparation Time 5 minutes

Cooking Time 1 hour 20-25 minutes

Peel the parsnips, finely slice the thinner ends and cut the thicker ends into quarters. Cut out the tough cores then thinly slice. Put them into a saucepan with the

milk(150ml) and cook for 20-25 minutes or until very soft. Put the cooked parsnips into a blender with about half of the cooking liquor and blend to a fine puree, adding a little milk if necessary. Return to a clean pan and add the cream and butter stirring. Season with salt and pepper (to taste) and leave over a gentle heat to keep warm until you are ready to serve.

Venison

Preparation Time 25 minutes

Cooking Time 11-13 minutes

Resting Time 10 minutes

Take the venison out of the fridge and allow to come up to room temperature for 20 minutes. Heat an ovenproof frying pan over a medium to high heat and add the oil. Season the meat with salt and pepper. When the oil is hot, add the meat and brown for 4-5 minutes. Turn to ensure an even colour. When nearly complete add the cold butter, turn down the heat to low and allow butter to melt without colour and use to baste the venison with a spoon being careful not to burn yourself. Put pan in oven and roast for 7-8

minutes for medium rare. The meat should feel slightly springy to touch. Remove from the pan, loosely cover with tin foil and rest in a warm place for about 10 minutes.

To serve

1. Heat a frying pan with a few drops of oil, add the gnocchi and place in a hot oven for about 10 minutes until you have a dark golden brown crust underneath. Then lift out the gnocchi and serve golden side up. (This should be done while cooking and resting the venison).

2. Gently warm the cabbage in a pan over a low heat and place a neat pile near the centre of the plate.

3. Place the roasted gnocchi next to the cabbage.

4. Spoon on the parsnip puree around the plate.

5. Slice the venison thickly and arrange over the cabbage.

6. Serve with a little red wine sauce or gravy and maybe some parsnip crisps to add height and texture to the dish.

Ingredients

- 250g rice
- 1 Onion finely chopped
- 1 Garlic clove crushed
- 1 Packet of butter
- 12.5g Dried ceps
- 625ml water
- 75ml White wine
- 1 Pinch dried thyme
- 250g Assorted cleaned wild New Forest mushrooms
- 100g butternut squash diced
- 50g Rosary goats cheese

Chopped parsley

- Grated Parmesan
- Pea shoots
- Salt & pepper

Butternut Squash Purée

- 1 Small butternut squash
- 3 Shallots finely chopped
- 2 Cloves crushed garlic
- 75g Butter
- 1 Pinch of dried thyme

Risotto of Butternut Squash, New Forest Wild Mushrooms and Rosary Goats Cheese

Method

Risotto

Make a mushroom stock by boiling the dried ceps in 625ml of water. Sweat the onion & garlic until soft with a little butter. Add the white wine and the dried thyme and reduce until almost dry. Add the rice and cook by adding a little stock at a time whilst stirring.

Butternut Squash Purée

Coat the squash in a little olive oil and roast in olive oil until softened. Sweat the shallots and garlic in butter in a pan add the squash and thyme and cook through. Blitz to a smooth

An English Original… *Chewton Glen* is a luxury country house hotel and spa set in 130 acres of countryside on the edge of the New Forest National Park, and just a few minutes' walk from the sea.

Vetiver restaurant offers a nexus of beautiful conservatories, intimate dining spaces and a stunning wine room. Vetiver is as formal or relaxed as the mood takes you. The menu has been created to celebrate old *Chewton Glen* favourites incuding Twice-Baked Emmental Soufflé and embrace an eclectic selection of new dishes.

Executive Head Chef Luke Matthews has been at *Chewton Glen* since 1993. He worked for ten years as Senior Sous Chef and in 2003 was appointed Executive Head Chef. Luke has honed his skills to develop a fabulous team and a well-recognised style of cuisine, whose secret lies in the quality of the ingredients selected and a deceptively simple approach to the preparation.

urée using a hand blender loosening with a plash of stock if needed.

o finish

ook the diced butternut squash in a pan with little butter until softened. Sweat the wild ushrooms in a pan with some butter. Add e butternut purée to the part-cooked risotto nd continue cooking out. Finish by adding e mushrooms, diced butternut, parmesan nd parsley. Garnish with the pea shoots and osary goat's cheese.

Poached Turbot

Ingredients

- 1 Whole Turbot approx 2kg in weight (ask your fishmonger to fillet it, and portion it for 4 people, keeping the frame)
- 200g peeled baby carrots (blanched in salted water until almost tender, refreshed in cold water)
- 200g trimmed baby leeks (blanched in salted water until almost tender, refreshed in cold water)
- 200g fresh peas
- 200g frozen broad beans (defrosted & de-pod
- 100g breakfast radishes (halved)
- 200g peeled baby new potatoes (cooked in some of the fish stock, keep warm)
- 1 bunch of chives (finely chopped)
- 1 bunch of parsley (finely Chopped)
- Juice of 1 lemon
- 4ltrs Purefoy Arms fish stock
- Ibiza Wild flower sea salt
- 1 bottle of white truffle oil

Method

1. Very gently bring the fish stock up to the simmer placing your fish in so its half submerged keeping the fish stock to a gentle simmer at all times
2. 1minute after add the potatoes.
3. 1 minute after that add the carrots, leeks & radishes
4. 1 minute after that add the broad beans and peas
5. Cover and simmer for a further 3 minutes
6. By this time the fish should be cooked and the vegetables warmed through and remaining bright green.
7. Add the parsley, chives and lemon juice
8. Divide equally into 4 main course bowls making sure you're generous with the stock
9. Sprinkle fish with the sea salt and drizzle with truffle oil
10. Serve with a nicely chilled Viognier

Ingredients

- 800g fish frames (removing gills and eyes, ask your fishmonger)
- 260g onion (2)
- 380g leek (2)
- 130g celery (2 sticks)
- 2 peeled cloves of garlic
- 2 bay leaves
- 1 small bunch of dill
- 1 small bunch of tarragon
- 1 sprig of thyme
- 1 teaspoon of peppercorns
- 5 litres of cold water

Purefoy Fish Stock

Method

1. Rinse the fish bones under cold, running water for about 10 minutes to remove any blood.

2. Peel the onion, and finely slice

3. Remove the root and the green of the leek and chop it with the celery into 5cm pieces.

4. Put fish bones into a large pot with the water and bring it to the boil.

5. When it starts to boil, turn it down to a low heat and remove the scum that floats to the surface. Then add all the other ingredients.

6. Simmer gently for 20 minutes.

7. Using a fine sieve, strain the liquid into a bowl. There will be a natural sediment from the bones that will have settled on the bottom of the pot. Making sure not to pour this through the sieve.

8. Discard all the bones, vegetables, herbs and the sediment in the pot.

9. Allow the stock to cool naturally and use as required.

Ingredients

- 2 (225g) fillets monkfish
- 2 tablespoons Naked Jam's lime marmalade
- 1 tablespoon chopped root ginger
- 1 tablespoon dark soy sauce
- 1 tablespoon rapeseed oil

Monkfish with Naked Jam Lime Marmalade

Method

1. Place the monkfish onto tin foil. In a bowl, whisk together the lime marmalade, root ginger and soy sauce. Pour the marinade over the fish and with another sheet of tin foil, fold the edges to form a parcel. Place in the fridge for 30 minutes to marinate.

2. Preheat the oven to 180°C / Gas 4. Grease a shallow baking dish with the rapeseed oil.

3. Transfer the fish and marinade to the prepared baking dish.

4. Bake in the preheated oven for about 20 minutes, until the flesh turns white and flakes

5. Serve on a bed of salad or with crushed new potatoes and fresh wilted greens. For an accompanying wine choose something like the Mâcon-Vergisson, La Roche, Nadine et Maurice Guerrin 2010

naked jam...

Naked jam is a Hampshire artisan producer of award winning jams and conserves that brings together a true understanding of flavour and quality. Using foraged and local ingredients combining traditional and modern ideas to jam making.

naked jam...

79

Newlyns Beef Stroganoff

Serves: 2

Preparation time:
15 minutes

Cooking time:
10-15 minutes

Ingredients

- 1tsp paprika (smoked can be used)
- 1tbsp oil
- 400g Newlyns beef fillet
- 1tbsp olive oil
- 20g butter
- 1 shallot, finely chopped
- 100g chestnut mushrooms
- 3tbsp brandy
- 1tbsp flour
- 1tsp tomato puree
- 150ml Newlyns beef stock
- 2tsp mustard
- 150ml sour cream or crème fraiche
- Flat leaf parsley to decorate

Newlyns Cookery School

Method

1. Rub the 1tbsp of oil and paprika into the beef slices and leave for 5 minutes.

2. Heat the 1tbsp of olive oil into a frying pan and then brown off the beef very quickly.

3. Remove with a slotted spoon.

4. In the same pan, add the butter, shallot and mushrooms and allow to soften.

5. Flambé with the brandy until evaporated.

6. Add the flour and tomato puree and cook for 1 minute.

7. Add the stock and reduce down until syrupy.

8. Add the sour cream, pour into a dish and sprinkle with flat leaf parsley.

We are a fourth generation farming family and passionate custodians of the local countryside. We opened *Newlyns Farm Shop* in 2004, offering customers a wide variety of free range meat which is reared on our farm and butchered by our in house resident butchers. Through this we are able to ensure full traceability of our meat.

Building on our desire to show people how to prepare and cook using our produce, we opened Newlyns Cookery School in 2008. Within the fantastically equipped kitchen situated above the farm shop, we share our culinary skills, techniques and knowledge to our customers.

We pride ourselves on showcasing to pupils how to get the best out of seasonal produce and the importance of treating the food with the respect it deserves. We inspire our customers to cook with passion as well as encouraging them to step out of their comfort zones with new ingredients and methods.

Medallions of Venison with Blackcurrant Glazed Beetroots and Potato Galette

Ingredients

- 500g Trimmed New Forest Venison Loin
- 12 x Rashers of Rindless Smoked Streaky Bacon
- 16 x Local Baby Beetroots (can be sourced from "Secretts")
- 100mls Blackcurrant Juice
- 50g Blackcurrants
- Fresh Oregano
- 4 x Medium Jacket Potatoes
- 100g Unsalted Butter
- Sunflower Oil
- 150mls Good Quality Veal or Beef Jus
- 125ml Port or Red Wine
- 1 x Banana Shallot
- ½ Stick Celery
- 1 x Medium Carrot
- Salt & Ground Black Pepper

Serves 4

Preparation Time 40 minutes after chilling venison in fridge

Method

1. Lay out a piece of cling film to about 40cm and fold width ways exactly in half

2. Arrange streaky bacon neatly vertically across the cling film, slightly overlapping

3. Lay the trimmed venison loin on the bacon, season with ground black pepper and a little salt (small amount of salt as the bacon is generally salty)

4. Roll the venison tightly in the cling film to form a sausage, twisting the ends to ensure as much air as possible is removed. Store in fridge for 1 to 4 hours

5. Peel and thinly slice potatoes (recommend use of a mandolin)

6. Gently melt butter

7. Brush rings with butter and arrange on a baking tray lined with silicone paper

8. Neatly arrange potato slices in the rings, brush with butter and lightly season

9. Continue process to fill rings finishing with butter

10. Cover with tin foil cook in oven for 35mins @ 160°c gas 3

11. Trim baby beetroots, roll in oil and bake in oven until cooked. Remove from oven and whilst warm gently peel off the skin

12. Finely chop shallots, celery and carrot

13. If using port - add jus and port together and gently reduce to 150mls with the chopped vegetables and sprig of oregano

14. If using red wine - you will need to reduce the red wine first before adding to jus and chopped vegetables

15. Check if the potato galette is cooked with a round ended knife (if knife goes through without resistance its cooked).

16. If so, turn oven up to 180°c and remove foil, lightly press the galette so the butter rises above the potato (this ensures the potato will be golden brown, not burnt) and place back in ove until golden brown

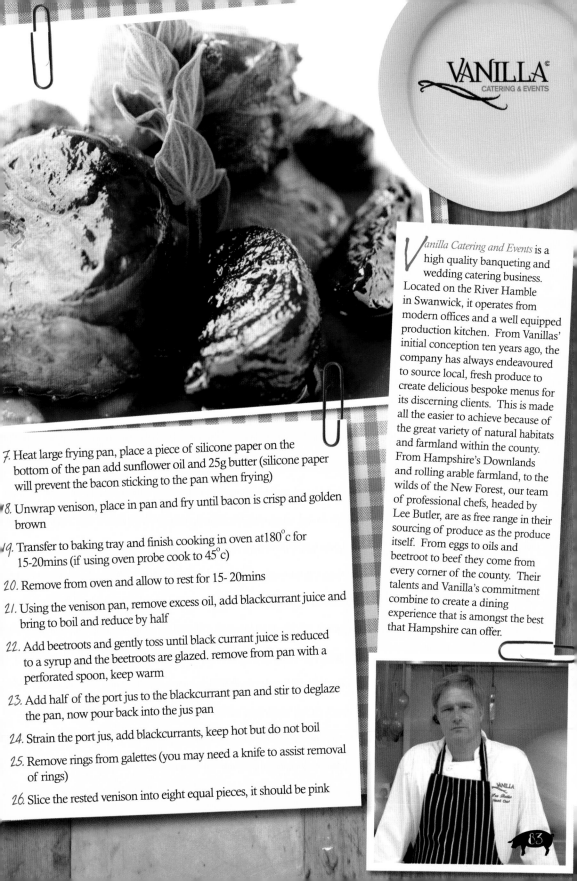

VANILLA
CATERING & EVENTS

7. Heat large frying pan, place a piece of silicone paper on the bottom of the pan add sunflower oil and 25g butter (silicone paper will prevent the bacon sticking to the pan when frying)

8. Unwrap venison, place in pan and fry until bacon is crisp and golden brown

9. Transfer to baking tray and finish cooking in oven at180°c for 15-20mins (if using oven probe cook to 45°c)

20. Remove from oven and allow to rest for 15- 20mins

21. Using the venison pan, remove excess oil, add blackcurrant juice and bring to boil and reduce by half

22. Add beetroots and gently toss until black currant juice is reduced to a syrup and the beetroots are glazed. remove from pan with a perforated spoon, keep warm

23. Add half of the port jus to the blackcurrant pan and stir to deglaze the pan, now pour back into the jus pan

24. Strain the port jus, add blackcurrants, keep hot but do not boil

25. Remove rings from galettes (you may need a knife to assist removal of rings)

26. Slice the rested venison into eight equal pieces, it should be pink

Fillet of River Test Trout served with Salad of Marinated Cucumber and White Wine Butter Sauce

Ingredients

- 4 fillets of River Test trout or 4 x150g pieces of a large salmon
- 4 tblsps of clarified butter
- 2 large cucumbers
- A large Isle of Wight Tomato
- 1 tblsps chopped fresh dill
- 200 ml white wine butter sauce
- Rock salt
- 150ml virgin olive oil

For the white wine butter sauce:

- 4 shallots finely chopped
- 100g unsalted butter (diced)
- 6 black peppercorns
- 30ml white wine vinegar
- 60 ml A Hampshire white wine such as: Wickham special release Fumé
- 30 ml double cream

Serves: 4

Method

1. Pour the clarified butter over the trout, sprinkle with a little salt and steam for about 4 minutes per trout fillet or 8-10 minutes for salmon

2. Meanwhile, peel the cucumber and cut into 1cm pieces, sprinkle with salt and drain in a colander.

3. Cut the tomato in quarters and remove the seeds and skin. Cut into small pieces and place in 4 tbsp of olive oil, warm slightly over the hob and set aside.

4. Wash the cucumber and plunge into boiling water for 5 seconds. Then toss the cucumber in 4 tbsp of olive oil with chopped fresh dill.

5. Spoon the cucumber into the middle of 4 warm plates and surround with the white wine butter sauce. Place the trout onto the cucumber and then pour over the tomatoes.

– Tylney Hall –

★★★★

A Victorian Grade II* listed house, *Tylney Hall* sits in 66 acres of rolling Hampshire countryside. With glorious grounds originally designed by renowned gardener, Gertrude Jekyll, a sense of calm is echoed throughout.

The level of comfort is typified by 112 bedrooms, all individually furnished. Palatial lounges offer the perfect location to enjoy a quiet drink or afternoon tea overlooking the gardens.

Award winning cuisine is served in the Oak Room Restaurant, where a modern cooking style with classic hallmarks combines with the best local produce.

The luxurious health spa offers the latest treatments, gymnasium, saunas plus indoor and outdoor pools. There is also an 18-hole golf course that neighbours the hotel.

With a range of private function rooms, Tylney Hall is a popular venue for weddings, meetings and events.

Tylney Hall is convenient for all travellers, being close to the M3 and M25, 40 minutes from Heathrow Airport and with good links into London.

For the White wine butter sauce:

1. Place the chopped shallots, peppercorns, white wine vinegar and white wine in a pan and reduce by 65%

2. Add the double cream, bring the mixture back to the boil and reduce for 1 minute.

3. Whisk in the diced butter gradually.

4. Serve warm and do not re-boil.

Slow Roast Free Range Pork Belly with Carrot Two Ways, Fondant Potato and Greens

Ingredients

- 1 Belly of free range pork (bones removed)

For the brine

- 160g salt
- 2L water
- 1 star anise
- Sage

Carrot pureé

- 8 medium carrots peeled and finely sliced
- 1 star anise
- 200g unsalted butter
- 300ml good quality chicken stock

Fondant potato

- 6 large Maris piper potatoes
- 150g unsalted butter

Roasted carrots

- 30 young organic carrots washed
- 2 cloves garlic
- 1 sprig thyme
- ½ orange (juiced)
- 2 star anise
- 100ml water
- Maldon sea salt

For the sauce

- 500ml reduced veal stock
- 100g unsalted butter
- 8 sage leaves finely chopped
- 50ml good quality sherry vinegar

Method

1. First brine the pork belly. Add the water, salt, herbs and spices to a pan and bring to the boil. Remove from the heat and allow to cool completely, then add the pork belly and refrigerate for 24 hours.

2. Next remove the belly from the brine and rinse under running cold water for 2-5 minutes, this removes excess brine. Pat dry with paper towel and place in a deep tray with greaseproof paper on the top and bottom. Add 500ml water and cover with foil, place in an oven preheated to 140°c for 4 ½ hours. After this time rub a little oil over the skin and increase the heat to 200°c to crackle the skin. This should take around 30 minutes.

3. Meanwhile prepare the garnish. For the fondants peel and wash the potatoes. Cut the side of each potato making it an even thickness. With a pastry cutter punch out a circle from the middle of each and rinse off excess starch under the tap. In a pan melt the butter and add the potatoes. Cook gently until the butter starts to turn brown. Once this stage is reached turn the potatoes to cook the other side. Check for doneness by inserting a small knife. (If the butter starts to brown too much add a splash of water) remove from the heat and set aside.

4. For the carrot puree, place the carrots in a medium pan with the anise and butter. Put them on the heat. Sweat the carrots in the butter until the moisture comes out, at this stage add the chicken stock. Increase the heat and boil until the carrots are tender it is important to not overcook to retain flavour. Plac

The Crown
a passion for food

into a liquidiser and puree until smooth, put into a bowl and cover the surface with cling film to stop a skin from forming.

5. To roast the carrots mix all ingredients together, place onto a baking tray and put into a 200°c oven for 25 minutes. Season with Maldon sea salt and set aside for later.

6. For the sauce, place the butter in a small pan and melt on a gentle heat, allow to reach a nut brown stage. Add the sage and the sherry vinegar; reduce the vinegar for 1minute. Add the veal stock and boil for 5 minutes.

7. To serve, on a warm plate pool the carrot pureé and sit the roasted carrots on top. Add some wilted seasonal greens and place the fondant potato on top, carve a portion of pork and sit on top of the carrots. Pour the sauce over the belly and serve!

Eating out is one of life's little pleasures. At *The Crown*, we take great pride in the fact that our chefs prepare every dish from scratch in our kitchen here in Old Basing. The preparation of your meal starts with the sourcing of the finest ingredients that Basingstoke, its surrounding areas and Britain have to offer and ends with the final flash in the pan at service

With a real passion for food *The Crown* is a village pub with a warm atmosphere and friendly service. In the kitchen you will find the Chef's, Chris Barnes and Tom Wilson, who create all of the dishes using the freshest ingredients from local suppliers.

Both Chef's have experience at Lainston House Hotel and have learned that there is nothing more important than creating a menu with a real emphasis on flavour. Everything is homemade, from the bread served at the beginning of the meal to the fudge that comes with your coffee.

Whether you are looking for a light bite in the bar or a 3 course meal in the restaurant *The Crown* has something for everyone.

James Goldings Game and Ox Kidney Pie

Ingredients

- 5kg of Assortment of Game i.e. Venison, Pigeon, Partridge and Hare
- 2/3kg of Ox Kidneys, fresh not frozen
- 2kg Onions, sliced
- 2ltr of Veal stock
- 1ltr of Chicken stock
- 300ml of Red Wine
- 200ml of Ringwood Forty niner Beer
- 25ml of Worcester Sauce
- 3 Bayleaves
- 3 Sprigs of Savoury or Thyme
- 15g of Beef Stock or Bouillon
- 50g Plain Flour
- Beef dripping
- Salt and Black Pepper
- *Optional* Chopped mixed herbs i.e. Marjoram, Rosemary or Sage

Method

1. Trim the game and cut into 2-3cm cubes
2. Peel and trim the kidneys and cut into triangle shape chunks
3. Heat two pans to "smoking point" and add dripping
4. Heat game and kidneys (separately) in seasoned flour
5. Seal in pans till colour starts to form
6. Slice the onions and cook to caramelised
7. Add bay and thyme, red wine
8. Deglaze for 2-3 mins
9. Add stocks and bring to boil, skim then cover with lid
10. Simmer until the game is tender (but still whole chunks)
11. Add the beer and Worcester Sauce, skim the mixture and then simmer for 10 mins
12. Check and adjust the seasoning and add optional herbs
13. Leave to cool in pot with lid ¾ on
14. Once cooled place in a baking dish, cover with savoury pastry & bake for 20-30mins at 180°C until golden

THE PIG

ROOMS &
KITCHEN GARDEN FOOD

Set in the heart of The New Forest, *The Pig* is a restaurant with rooms; the focus is very much on the food; uncomplicated and simple British garden food, true to the micro seasons and influenced by the forest. Everything is driven by the gardener, forager and chef - they grow and find the food, the Head Chef James Golding then creates the 25-mile menu (what we can't get from our kitchen garden and grounds is sourced locally). This immediacy from garden to plate is *The Pig's* trademark!

Home grown in every way; our 26 bedroom country house in Brockenhurst is original, relaxed and sitting comfortably within its environment. It isn't perfect! but it's comfy, interesting and homely with muted colours, a bit shabby chic, evolved rather than interior designed – a touch of luxury combined with a homely charm!

Dan's Herbed Rack of Lamb with Cherry Jus

Ingredients

Cherry Jus

- 150g semi dried or fresh cherries, stoned
- 450ml red wine
- 2 garlic cloves, peeled & chopped
- 1 shallot, peeled & diced
- 250ml chicken stock
- 25g butter
- Seasoning

Lamb

- 2 Newlyns Farm lamb racks
- 1 tbsp English mustard
- 3 slices stale bread
- 4 tbsp Lyburn Winchester Mature Cheese
- Herbs - small bunch of parsley, thyme, coriander, rosemary
- 1 tbsp Pratts Rapeseed oil

Serves 2

Method

Cherry Jus

1. Put cherries, wine, garlic and shallot into a saucepan. Cook for 10 minutes using a high heat, mixture should reduce until almost dry.

2. Reduce the heat, add the stock and cook for 15 -20 minutes until the sauce is thick. Whisk in the butter, season and keep warm.

Lamb

1. Pre heat oven 200°C Gas mark 6

2. Using a sharp knife remove the skin from the lamb racks and score the fat. Brush with the mustard.

3. Place bread into a food processor, and pulse for 1 minute. Add the cheese, herbs and a ½ spoon of oil. Pulse for 1 minute until blended, add more oil if dry.

4. Coat the lamb completely with the herb and cheese mix.

5. Place on a baking sheet and cook for 12 – 15 mins. Remove from the oven cover with foil and leave to rest for 10 minutes.

6. Serve lamb with warm cherry jus and seasonal vegetables. Dan served a courgette and potato rosti cake and Hampshire asparagus with his lamb.

CREATE & Cook COMPETITION 2014

The Create & Cook Competition is a fun, innovative cookery competition for young cooks aged 12-14 in Hampshire secondary schools. It is run by fit2cook food education and sponsored by The Southern Co-operative. The aims of the Competition are to nurture young talent and celebrate local food. Young cooks have to design a two course menu using as many Hampshire ingredients as possible and they have to fill in a questionnaire about their local produce. This encourages them to think about how their food is produced and the advantages of buying local - sustainability, food miles and supporting local farmers and food producers. The Competition in Hampshire is supported by Hampshire Fare, Hampshire Farmers Markets, Lainston House Hotel, Newlyns Farm Cookery School and Highbury College. Now in its fifth year the Competition has discovered dozens of fantastic young cooks all with a passion for creating menus that have a flavour of where they live.

Dan is a student at Robert May's School, Odiham To find out more and how to enter the 2014 Competition please see www.fit2cook.co.uk/createandcook

Fit2Cook FOOD EDUCATION

The Southern Co-operative

91

Hampshire Pheasant Cooked in a Mediterranean Style

The county of Hampshire is one of the most wooded in England and provides a rich harvest of wild game. A brace of pheasants can be bought cheaply from local butchers or at one of the many farmers' markets throughout the autumn and winter. It is completely organic and free from fat and cholesterol. This recipe combines the delicious taste of pheasant with the tastes and colours of the Mediterranean. It is a delicious one pot supper dish, requiring no accompaniments, and can be taken straight from the oven and served to guests.

Serves: 6

Ingredients

- A brace of pheasant, skinned and quartered (the butcher will do this for you)
- Brown basmati rice measured into a 225ml measuring jug
- 2 large red peppers
- 300ml of chicken stock
- 2 medium onions
- 150ml of dry white wine
- 50g of sun-dried tomatoes in olive oil
- 1 tablespoon of tomato puree
- 2-3 tablespoons of olive oil
- 1 teaspoon of paprika
- 2 cloves of chopped/crushed garlic
- A level teaspoon of mixed dried herbs
- 150g of chorizo cut into 1cm cubes
- 50g of black olives, stoned and cut in half
- Salt and ground black pepper
- 1 large orange cut into 8 wedges and peeled
- A heavy 4ltr ovenproof casserole pan with a tight fitting lid

Method

1. Start off by seasoning the pheasant joints well with salt and pepper.

2. Next slice the red peppers in half and remove the seeds and pith, then slice each half into bite sized pieces. Peel the onion and slice into strips of approximately the same size.

3. The sun-dried tomatoes should be drained, wiped dry with kitchen paper and then cut into 1cm pieces.

4. Heat 2 tablespoons of olive oil in the casserole and, when it is fairly hot, add the pheasant pieces - two or three at a time - and brown them to a nutty golden colour on both sides. Once they are brown, remove them to a plate with a draining-spoon. Next add a little more oil to the casserole, turn down the heat a little and add the onion and peppers and allow them to brown a little at the edges, moving them around from time to time, for about 5 minutes.

5. Add the garlic, chorizo and dried tomatoes and cook these for a minute or two until the garlic is pale golden and the chorizo has taken on some colour.

6. Stir in the rice and, when the grains have a good coating of oil, add the stock, wine, tomato puree and paprika.

BRIDGEFAST
property services

*A*re you thinking of selling your property? Do you need funding in advance of selling your property? *Bridgefast* offers a complete managed service in respect of the sale of property for retired homeowners. We manage the whole process including liaising with estate agents and solicitors on behalf of our clients, each of whom is assigned a personal adviser who is in communication with them throughout the process. In addition to this service, Bridgefast will also arrange and manage other property related services for our clients such as removals, house clearance and cleaning. All these additional services are offered at cost.

Importantly, *Bridgefast* can offer our clients access to flexible funding prior to their property being sold. They can then use this to pay for monthly nursing or care home fees, an immediate care plan, a downsizing bridge, property deposit or rent.

7. As soon as everything has reached simmering point, turn the heat down to a gentle simmer. Add a little more seasoning, then place the pheasant pieces back into the pan.

8. The rice has to stay in the liquid to cook. Sprinkle in the herbs and olives and arrange the wedges of orange on top.

9. Cover with a tight fitting lid and cook in a pre-heated oven at 180°C for an hour. Serve straight from the oven.

Stuffed Beefsteak Tomatoes

Serves: 4 as a main dish

Preparation Time Approximately 10 minutes

Cooking Time Approximately 50 minutes

Method

1. Preheat the oven to 190C/gas mark 5. Remove the top 2cm of each beefsteak tomato. Extract the seeds and pulp and set aside in a bowl, ensuring you do not damage the outer edges of the tomatoes.

2. Fry the onion and garlic on a medium heat, allowing them to soften but not to brown. Add the tomato pulp to the pan and increase the heat slightly. Simmer for approximately 10 minutes. Add the vegetable stock and the rice, cover and leave to cook for around ten minutes before stirring in the basil, lemon zest and cheese. Season to taste.

3. Place the hollowed out beefsteak tomatoes on to a lightly oiled baking tray and carefully spoon the rice mixture in, leaving enough room to replace the tops. Bake the tomatoes into the oven for 25-30 minutes, until the tomato flesh is tender and the rice is fully cooked.

4. Decorate with fresh basil leaves and serve with a crisp mixed salad of your choice.

Ingredients

- 8 large beefsteak tomatoes
- 1 small onion, diced
- 2 cloves of garlic, crushed
- 4 tbsp olive oil
- 150g easy-cook basmati rice
- 300ml hot vegetable stock
- 15g fresh basil leaves finely chopped, save a few leaves for garnish
- The finely grated zest of ½ a lemon
- 35g grated mature cheddar cheese
- Mixed salad to serve

the tomato stall.

*P*urveyors of delicious tomatoes grown with love on the sunny Isle of Wight specialising in bold, fresh flavours and 100% pure tomato inspired products. Discover award winning sauces, tomato juices and dressings made with only the finest ingredients and totally additive free.

Oak Smoked Salmon, New Potatoes, Avocado, Horseradish, Pickled Cucumber, Brown Shrimp and Caper Vinaigrette

Ingredients

Cured Salmon
- 500g Salmon Fillet
- 250g Rock Salt
- 200g Sugar
- 50g Mixed Crushed White and Black Pepper
- 5g Coriander Seeds
- 5 Cloves
- Juice and Zest from 1 Lemon & Lime
- 1 Bunch of Chopped Dill
- Couple of handful of oak smoking chips

Marinated new potatoes
- 100ml white wine vinegar
- 400ml olive oil
- salt to taste
- 8 new potatoes

Avocado puree
- 1 ripe Hass avocado
- Juice from 1/2 a lemon
- 1 tablespoon of crème fraiche
- Salt to taste

Horseradish crème fraiche
- 2 tablespoons horseradish sauce
- 100g crème fraiche

Pickled cucumbers
- 250ml muscatel vinegar
- 200ml white wine vinegar
- 200g caster sugar
- 1 star anise
- 4 cloves
- 1 tsp mustard seeds
- 1 cucumber

Serves 4

Preparation Time 6/8 hours

Cooking Time 30 minutes

Method

Smoked salmon:

1. Mix all of the ingredients together thoroughly then cover the salmon in a tray, wrap up and refrigerate for 6 - 8 hours to cure. When cured remove the salmon from the salt mix and wash under a cold tap removing all the excess cure mix then pat dry with a kitchen cloth.

2. Use a smoker or a metal steamer. Sprinkle wood chips in the bottom of the pan put the steamer basket with the salmon in and the lid on. Heat on a high flame until the chips start to smoulder and smoke remove from the heat and allow to smoke until the fish starts to cook, approximately 5-6 minutes if it needs more smoke just return it to the heat briefly. While the salmon is warm carefully flake it apart onto a tray then chill in the fridge until ready to serve.

New potatoes:

Boil the new potatoes in salted water until cooked then slice into quarters or half depending on the size. Blend the vinegar and oil together to make a vinaigrette, season with a touch of salt then add the cooked new potatoes while they are still warm.

Avocado puree:

Peel and remove the stone place all the ingredients into a blender and blend until smooth.

The Plough Inn
Longparish

*S*Dating back to 1721, *The Plough Inn* is in the beautiful village of Longparish in the picturesque Test Valley, close to the A303 and a short drive from Winchester, Basingstoke and Newbury. With the world renowned River Test on our doorstep and the Test Way passing through our car park, we provide the perfect stop for a refreshing pint of real ale and a bite from our delicious menu.

Taken over in April 2012 by renowned chef James Durrant, this remains a traditional country pub with a contemporary feel serving award winning food. The warm, welcoming surroundings, log burning fires and cosy snug retain the original character and charm. Our aim is to make guests feel welcome and comfortable whether for a quick drink or meeting with friends and family for lunch or dinner. There is plenty of room in our attractive garden for pub-catered picnics or for dining al fresco.

Horseradish creme fraiche:
In a bowl whisk the two ingredients together.

Pickle cucumber
Mix all of the ingredients apart from the cucumber together in a pan, bring to the boil then cool. Cut the cucumber into thick slices and submerge in the pickling liquor for 5 - 10 minutes.

Shrimp and caper vinaigrette:
Strain the vinaigrette from the potatoes and mix with the capers and the shrimps.

To dress:
Firstly arrange the salmon on the plate add dots of the avocado using a squeezy bottle or piping bag arrange the potatoes and cucumber around the plate drizzle with the horseradish the sprinkle over the capers and shrimps finish with some fresh sprigs of dill and watercress.

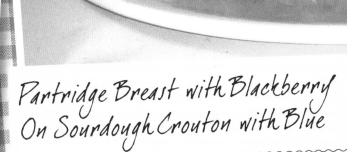

Ingredients

- 4 tablespoons Wild Island Blackberry Balsamic
- 4 Brownrigg Partridge Breasts
- 1 tablespoon Oil of Wight cold pressed rapeseed oil
- 50g crumbled IOW Blue Cheese
- 4 slices Island Bakers Sourdough Bread
- 6 Blackberries
- 2 Pears
- 3 handfuls Fresh Spinach and Rocket
- Freshly ground black pepper

Partridge Breast with Blackberry On Sourdough Crouton with Blue

This particular recipe as well as giving a taste of the Isle of Wight in Autumn and indeed Christmas with the nickname 'Partridge in a Pear tree' also showcases the Wild Island Blackberry Balsamic which was awarded 2 stars with the Great Taste judges commenting that it excels as a fruit vinegar "A great amount of blackberry on the nose, very well balanced with the balsamic not too acidic, leaving the blackberry to sing

Method

1. Heat griddle pan

2. Slice sourdough on the diagonal, brush with a little rapeseed oil. Griddle for a couple of minutes each side and remove from pan.

3. Slice pears into 6 lengthways, core then griddle until tender and remove

Wild Island is based on Provenance, Quality and Taste. It was founded in 2011 with a mission of promoting the use of local produce to create quality infused oils, fruit vinegars, marinades and dressings, in turn promoting local farmers, producers and the great flavours of the Isle of Wight.

Designed to add an extra dimension to culinary creations, encouraging customers to mix and match products, bringing a little alchemy into the kitchen.

The bottles are designed for reuse with imaginative ideas such as homemade raspberry lemonade or liqueurs to make original gifts. Every bottle also has a range of enticing recipe ideas on the label.

Balsamic cheese and Griddled Pears *Serves:* 4

4. Prepare salad leaves and arrange on serving plates

5. Place griddled sourdough on each

6. Season partridge breasts with freshly ground black pepper

7. Heat a little more oil in pan and pan fry partridge breasts for 2 -3 minutes each side (depending on how rare you would like them)

8. Remove from pan and arrange on top of sourdough along with the pears and blackberries.

9. Crumble IOW blue cheese over.

10. Return pan to the heat and add Blackberry Balsamic. Allow to bubble and reduce slightly

11. Drizzle over et voila!

Dee Chauhan

Rosemary Lamb Crumble

Serves: 4 *Preparation Time:* 20 minutes
Cooking Time: 20 minutes

Ingredients

- 40ml rapeseed oil
- 60g torn bread of choice
- 24g rolled oats
- 60g Lyburn's Winchester cheese or medium cheddar cheese, grated
- 4 sprigs of fresh rosemary, chopped
- 45ml (3 tbsp) rapeseed oil
- 1 large onion, peeled and finely chopped
- 1½ tsp garlic paste (chesnok wight)
- 450g (1lb) Laverstoke Park lean organic minced lamb
- 1 leek, trimmed and sliced
- 2 medium carrots, diced
- 300 ml lamb or vegetable stock
- 2 tbsp tomato purée
- 1 tbsp Worcestershire sauce
- ½ tbsp corn flour, blended with a little cold water
- Salt and freshly ground black pepper for seasoning

Method

1. Preheat the oven to 190°C 375°F Gas Mark 5
2. Mix all the crumble ingredients in a food blender or with your fingers to create a coarse crumble mix. Refrigerate.
3. Heat the oil in a large pan, ideally a sauté pan on a medium heat.
4. Add onions and stir often. When the onions start to turn a light golden brown add the garlic paste and reduce heat and cook for 2 minutes.
5. Now add the minced lamb stirring all the time preventing chunky nuggets of meat.
6. On a medium heat let the lamb brown for about 5-8 minutes so that it seals and browns whilst taking on the lovely garlic flavour. Mix in the leek and carrot, cook for two minutes.
7. Pour in the stock, add tomato puree and Worcestershire sauce. Bring to the boil, then reduce the heat, cover and simmer for about 5 minutes stirring half way through.
8. Stir the blended corn-flour into the mince mixture, cook for a further 1-2 minutes until thickened, then season with salt and pepper.
9. Transfer to a shallow ovenproof baking dish. Sprinkle the crumble mixture evenly onto the lamb filling.
10. Bake in a pre-heated oven for 20 minutes or until the topping is crispy and golden in colour.
11. Serve immediately; ideally with steamed seasonal vegetables.

Fyffes Banoffi Pie

Serves: 8

Preparation time: 15–20 minutes

Chilling time: 2–3 hours

Ingredients

For the base
- 275g unsalted butter
- 225g digestive biscuits, crushed
- 1/2 tsp ground ginger or ground cinnamon

For the filling
- 1 x 400g can of sweetened condensed milk
- 150g caster sugar
- 3 bananas, peeled
- 225ml double cream, lightly whipped

To decorate
- 3tbsps grated chocolate

Method

1. Melt 100g/4oz butter in a pan over a gentle heat. Take off the heat and stir in the biscuits and spice.

2. Press the biscuit mixture around the sides and base of a loose-based flan tin. Chill for 20 – 30 minutes until set.

3. In a non-stick medium pan put the milk, sugar and remaining butter. Over a very gentle heat dissolve the sugar before bringing up to the boil, stirring all the time. Stir until the mixture turns a pale golden brown colour, then pour into the prepared case. Leave to set (cold).

4. Slice the bananas and arrange half on top of the caramel. Put a quarter of the bananas into the whipped cream and spread on top of the caramel layer.

5. Decorate with the remaining bananas and grated chocolate. Serve in slices.

Top tip

The secret to a perfect caramel is to cook it slowly and make sure you stir the mixture all the time. If you don't, it will get stuck on the base of the pan and the mixture will have brown flecks in it

*F*yffes - we're famous for our bananas. When Edward Fyffe brought his first few bunches over from the Canary Islands in September 1888, little could he have imagined that his banana business would grow to become the UK number 1 and the biggest Fairtrade Banana supplier to Europe. We've branched out too and the *Fyffes* Blue Label, first applied in 1929, now also appears on top quality supersweet pineapples.

And we still do things differently from our big international contemporaries. Rather than buy-up vast plantations, we prefer to work with local growers to help them get their produce to market. Our relationship with the growers in Belize for example, stretches back 40 years.

From our UK head office in Basingstoke, we're delighted to be able to support The Princes Trust by sponsoring this fabulous recipe for Fyffes Banoffi Pie – hope you enjoy it!

Laverstoke Park Farms Buffalo Milk Croissant Bread and Butter Pudding

Ingredients

- 500ml Laverstoke Park Buffalo Milk
- 6 Organic Laverstoke Park Egg Yolks
- 100g Sugar
- 1 Vanilla Pod
- 4 Croissants (sliced) - day old are best
- Softened butter
- 60g Sultanas
- Sugar to Glaze

Method

1. Lightly butter the croissant slices and layer into a dish, sprinkle with the sultanas and top with the remaining croissant slices.

2. Pour the buffalo milk onto to a medium-sized saucepan. Split the vanilla pod lengthways and scrape out the seeds. Add the pod and seeds to the milk and bring to a gentle boil.

3. In a separate bowl, whisk the egg yolks and sugar together until well creamed and the sugar is dissolved.

4. Pour the boiled milk over the egg yolks and sugar and whisk well. Pass the custard mixture through a fine sieve over the croissant slices.

5. Sit the dish into a warm water bath (bain-marie), cover with foil and place in a pre-heated oven (120-150°C Gas Mark 2-3).

6. Cook for 30-40 minutes until the pudding is just set. Remove from the oven, sprinkle with icing or caster sugar and glaze under a hot grill immediately before serving.

LAVERSTOKE PARK FARM

Laverstoke Park Farm was founded in 1996 by former Formula One World Champion, Jody Scheckter, with the principle to create "the best tasting healthiest food without compromise".

Today Laverstoke leads the way in Biodynamic and Organic farming in the UK, with the major emphasis on the health of the soil and slow-growing animals as the key to both sustainable farming and the best tasting produce.

Laverstoke's produce really is second to none. Amongst the many award winning products the farm has become famous for is the Laverstoke buffalo mozzarella which is made with the milk from the 2,000 strong herd of buffalo. The farm's herd also provides its rich milk to make delicious ice-creams, yoghurt, brie and burrata.

In addition to the unique and exciting selection of dairy products, Laverstoke produces both classic and more unusual sausages, burgers, pies, biltong and much more. All available online or at the farm shop near Overton, its Twickenham based farm shop as well as selected retailers.

Jude's Zesty Apricot and Almond tart with Ginger Ice Cream

Ingredients

Base
- 225g plain flour
- 110g unsalted butter (room temperature)
- 80g caster sugar
- Zest of 1 lemon
- Pinch of salt

Almond Mix
- 100g caster
- 75g unsalted butter
- 3 of Jude's hen's eggs (they're usually slightly erratic in size but medium will do!)
- 150g ground almond
- 1 punnet of apricots (can used tinned if not in season)
- Juice of 1 lemon
- 1 tbsp of icing sugar

Final flourishes
- Apricot jam to glaze
- Flaked almonds to decorate
- Jude's Ginger Spice ice cream to serve

Method

1. Preheat your oven at 170 degrees. Butter 20cm deep fluted tart tin.

2. .Half and stone the apricots and place in a bowl with the juice of half of the lemon and a tablespoon of icing sugar. Leave apricots to absorb the lemon and sugar.

3. For the base. Crumb the flour and butter until well mixed. Add the sugar. Then beat in the egg. Mix altogether to form a soft smooth dough. If you need to loosen do so with a little milk (water will do if someone has pinched the last of the milk!) Then wrap the bowl in cling film and leave to chill for 30 minutes in the fridge.

4. For the mix. While the dough is chilling; beat the sugar and butter together until well incorporated. Stir in the ground almonds. Pour in the other half of the juice of the lemon. Then beat in each egg one at a time.

5. Remove the dough from the fridge and roll out (using icing sugar if the dough is a little wet). Roll out a line layer to line the base and sides. Put another small pie tin on top of the lined base (to keep it from rising in the oven) and put into the oven for 25 minutes.

6. Remove from oven and remove the second pie tin from on top of the pastry. Pour the almond mix into the pastry shell. Push the soaked apricot halves into the top of the mix and then sprinkle with flaked almonds to finish.

7. Leave in oven at the same temperature for 40 minutes. After 30 minutes take out of the oven and using a brush glaze the tart generously with apricot jam (it's worth that extra step as it gives the dish a beautiful glossy finish!) Return to oven for the final 10 minutes.

8. Leave to cool slightly and then serve with a generous scoop of Jude's Ginger Spice ice cream.

We're a small family company making a premium dairy ice cream in the village of Twyford, Hampshire. It all started with Jude's husband who dreamed of making the tastiest ice cream. He mixed and churned away in his small dairy barn and soon the whole family joined in. He lovingly named it Jude's after his wife.

At *Jude's* we love great flavours and source many of our ingredients locally. We use Hill farm's apples in our Apple sorbet and we love Summerdown Farm's Black Mitcham Peppermint in our Mint Choc Chip ice cream.

We now supply some of the best restaurants in the UK and have worked with some of Britain's top chefs. Jude's husband still develops our recipes... of all the flavours we've made Very Vanilla is still his favourite!

Top tip

Why not use any leftover dough to make mini versions in a muffin tray.

New Forest Gateau

Ingredients

For the Sponges
- 9 Medium Free Range Eggs
- 200g Golden Caster Sugar
- 90g Cocoa powder

For the Filling
- 425g can Pitted Cherries, drained with 2 tbsp juice reserved, rest drained
- 50g Kirsch (for a non alcoholic gateau, replace Kirsch with Cherry Juice)
- 500ml Double Cream
- 3tbsp Icing Sugar
- 125g Plain Chocolate
- A handful of fresh cherries

Method

1. Preheat oven to 180°C/Gas 4
2. Grease and line the base of 3 x 20cm cake tins
3. Separate the egg yolks and whites
4. Place in a bowl, using an electric whisk or food processor, whisk the egg yolks and sugar to a thick mousse-like consistency; you can test this by drizzling a little of the mixture over the rest, if the drizzled mixture holds its shape, it is ready.
5. Sift the cocoa and gently fold in with a metal spoon.
6. Place the egg whites into a clean bowl and whisk until stiff peaks form
7. Gently and slowly fold in half the yolk mixture, adding the remaining half when the first half has been fully combined
8. Divide the mixture between the 3 lined sandwich tins
9. Bake in for 15 minutes, swapping the tins over on the shelves to ensure each section cooks evenly
10. To test when the cakes are done, gently push in a skewer or sharp knife; if it comes out clean, the cakes are ready
11. Remove each cake from its tin and place on a wire rack
12. Prick the cakes a few times with a skewer or fork
13. Mix together the 2 tbsp reserved cherry juice and the kirsch (or more juice) and drizzle over the cakes
14. Leave to cool
15. Meanwhile Tip 200ml of the cream into a small pan and heat until just below simmering point. Chop 125g of the chocolate and put in a heatproof bowl, pour over the hot cream and stir until melted. Set aside until spreadable
16. When the cakes are cool whisk the remaining cream and the icing sugar together until softly whipped. Spread over two of the cakes and then spoon over the cherries. Stack the cakes together.
17. Spread the chocolate cream over the third cake and sit on top of the other cakes. Pile the fresh cherries in and around the cake and serve

hcr

H CR is a global Relocation Management Company with its HQ based in Basingstoke, a branch in Florida and a world connect network of partners. Since 1982 we have been looking after people by providing breakthrough mobility solutions for our clients. Whether you relocate one employee or hundreds of employees, whether they move domestically or internationally, over the short term or long term, permanently or are returning home for good – *HCR*, a carbon neutral company, can help you have the right people in the right place at the right time without it costing the earth.

Ingredients

Pastry
- 112g butter
- 112g sugar
- 1 egg
- 224g flour
- ½ vanilla pod
- 1 teaspoon of jam
- 1 scoop of clotted cream ice-cream

Frangipane
- 56g butter
- 56g sugar
- 56g ground almonds
- 28g self raising flour
- 1egg

Flaked Almond Bakewell Tart with Clotted Cream Ice Cream

Method

Pastry
1. Cream together butter and sugar with an electric whisk.
2. Add the egg and the vanilla seeds to the mixture.
3. Add the flour and mix till the pastry has come together.
4. Wrap the pastry dough in cling film and pop into the fridge.
5. Leave the pastry to rest for 2 hours.

Frangipane
1. Cream together butter and sugar with an electric whisk.
2. Add the egg and mix until smooth.
3. Add the almonds and flour until you have incorporated all the ingredients together.

S et in the heart of Romsey, *The White Horse* has been a Coaching Inn for over 600 years. A stay here is a time to unwind, savouring some of the finest food in Hampshire in our 2 AA Rosette Brasserie. Relax in one of the hotel's 31 individually designed bedrooms and suites and enjoy a drink or Afternoon Tea in the delightful Silks Bar or frescoed Tudor Lounge.

To make tartlets

1. Roll out the sweet pastry on a floured surface.

2. Grease and flour 2 circular moulds

3. Cut 2 disks in the pastry, line the moulds and leave a 1 cm over hang for cooking.

4. Rest the pastry in the fridge for 1 hour.

5. Blind bake the pastry tartlets at 170°c for 15 minutes.

6. Allow to cool and add 1 teaspoon of jam to the bottom of the tart.

7. Pipe or spoon in the frangipane ¾ of the way to the top.

8. Bake at 170°c for 15 minutes until the frangipane is cooked.

9. Remove from the oven and allow to cool and trim off the excess pastry.

10. Remove mould and top with warm toasted almonds.

11. Finish by dusting with icing sugar.

To Serve

1. Place a small spoonful of jam on one side of the plate and drag across to the other side with the back of a spoon.

2. Sit the bakewell on one side of the plate and sprinkle some crushed digestive biscuits next to it.

3. With an ice cream scoop take one ball of clotted cream ice cream and sit on top of the crushed biscuits.

Rocky Road with Oreo Cookies

Method

1. Heat the butter, chocolate and golden syrup in a heavy-based saucepan over a gentle heat. Remove from the heat, scoop out about 125ml/4½fl oz of the melted mixture and set aside in a bowl.

2. Place the biscuits into a plastic freezer bag and crush them with a rolling pin until some have turned to crumbs but there are still pieces of biscuit remaining.

3. Fold the biscuit pieces and crumbs into the melted chocolate mixture in the saucepan, then add the marshmallows and Oreos.

4. Tip the mixture into a 24cm/9in square baking tin and smooth the top with a wet spatula.

5. Pour over the reserved 125ml/4½fl oz of the melted chocolate mixture and smooth the top with a wet spatula.

6. Refrigerate for a minimum of 2 hours.

7. To serve, cut into portions and dust with icing sugar.

Ingredients

- 125g/4½oz soft unsalted butter
- 400g/10½oz best-quality dark chocolate, broken into pieces
- 3 tbsp golden syrup
- 100g/7¼oz digestive biscuits
- 150g Oreo cookies
- 100g/3½oz mini marshmallows
- 2 tsp icing sugar, to dust

Belinda Clark Marshmallows

Ingredients

- 300 grams granulated sugar
- 140 grams glucose
- 7 grams gelatine
- 100 grams raspberry puree (sieved you can make this from fresh or frozen raspberries)
- 8 tablespoons of cornflour
- 2 tablespoons of icing sugar
- 2 tablespoons of freeze-dried raspberry powder

Method

1. Lightly oil a 20cm x 20cm tin.

2. Mix the gelatine in the bowl of a stand mixer with the raspberry puree. (You can use a bowl and an electric hand whisk instead of a stand mixer but be warned – it takes a lot of whisking!)

3. Put the sugar in a pan with the glucose and add 100ml cold water. Set on the hob on a medium heat and bring it up to boiling point. Boil until it reaches the soft ball stage 115°C then turn off the heat and leave to cool to 100°C.

4. Add the hot sugar syrup to the gelatine and puree and stir gently. Whisk on a medium speed until the mixture starts to thicken, then turn the speed up to high. Continue whisking until the mixture is a pale-medium pink colour and thick enough to drop slowly off the whisk.

5. Pour in to the tin, spread out with a spatula and leave to set for at least 8 hours or overnight. (Taste the batter – it's delicious!)

6. Mix the cornflour, icing sugar and freeze-dried raspberry powder together and spread out on a work surface. Spread some of the powder over the top of your marshmallow and then turn it out of the tin. Cut in to cubes and roll in the powder.

Mitcham Mint Chocolate Ice Cream

Ingredients

- 300ml milk
- 300ml double cream
- 4 large egg yolks
- 75g caster sugar
- 1 tsp custard powder
- 100g Summerdown Mint Crisps, plus extra to serve

Top tip

This recipe is a firm favourite for people of all ages. Serve piled high in an ice cream cone for children on a hot summer's afternoon.

Method

1. Gently heat the milk and cream in a saucepan until it reaches simmering point.
2. Whisk the egg yolks with the sugar and custard powder until pale and thick then, still whisking, incorporate the hot cream.
3. Pour back into the saucepan and cook over a low heat, stirring constantly until it thickens. Transfer back into the mixing bowl and chill.
4. Chop the mint crisps into small pieces and stir into the cold custard.
5. To get the best texture, churn the mixture in an ice cream maker. Alternatively, pour the mixture into a tupperware container and freeze for 2 hours. When ice crystals start to form around the outside, whisk with an electric whisk until smooth. Freeze for another 2 hours, then whisk again. Repeat until firm and smooth.
6. Scoop the ice cream into glasses or bowls and serve with another mint crisp or two.

Top tip

Using a tsp of custard powder helps to stabilise the custard so there's less risk of the mixture splitting. You could also use cornflour which would do the same job.

Summerdown

S ummerdown grows and harvests the rare traditional Black Mitcham peppermint and distils its pure mint oil. It is then used to make their delicious Chocolate Peppermint Crisps, Peppermint Creams and refreshing Peppermint Tea.

At the beginning of the 20th century, England was renowned for producing the best mint in the world. Over the years, the rising cost of labour brought a decline in cultivation, but *Summerdown* has now reintroduced traditional Black Mitcham peppermint to this country. Throughout the area there are similar stories about heirloom varieties of fruit and rare breeds of meat. Support local producers and help keep our food heritage alive.

Ingredients

- 150g Butter, softened
- 2 large Bramley Apples, peeled, cored and sliced.
- 225g Doves Gluten Free Self- Raising Flour
- 225g Caster Sugar
- 1 teasp Wheat Free Baking Powder
- 2 Large Free Range Eggs, beaten
- 1/2 teasp French Almond Extract
- 30g Flaked Almonds

Hampshire Apple Cake (Gluten Free)

Method

1. Oven Temperature: Gas mark 3; 160°C; 140°C fan oven

2. Grease and line a 20cm loose bottomed cake tin.

3. Sieve flour and baking powder into a bowl.

GILBERT
WHITE'S
HOUSE
& GARDEN
and
THE OATES
COLLECTION

*G*ilbert White's House & Garden and The Oates Collection is situated in the heart of the pretty Hampshire village of Selborne. The 30 acres of garden and parkland are set against the backdrop of the magnificent beech clad hanger.

Visitors can enjoy a combined admission ticket to the House, Garden and Oates Collection. Discover the home of Gilbert White, pioneering 18th century explorer of the natural world. Explore The Oates Collection, interactive galleries tell the story of Captain Lawrence Oates of the Scott Antarctic Expedition. Learn about Frank Oates, Victorian naturalist and explorer who travelled widely in the Americas and in Africa.

Delicious refreshments, many locally sourced, are served in the Award-Winning Tea Parlour and delightful gifts can be found in the excellent Gift Shop. Visit us for a true taste of Hampshire!

Add sugar, beaten eggs, almond extract and butter and mix well.

Spread half the mixture in the tin and arrange the apple slices on top. Cover the apple slices with the remainder of the mixture. Sprinkle over the flaked almonds.

Bake for 1 to 1 1/2 hours depending on your oven. Cake should be golden brown when cooked. Serve warm with creme fraiche.

Chris's Gooseberry Cream Profiteroles

Serves 2

Ingredients

Profiteroles

- 100g strong plain flour
- 50g butter, cubed
- 4tbsp milk
- 4tbsp water
- 1 tsp caster sugar
- Pinch salt
- 3 large Claytons eggs, beaten
- 150g white chocolate

Filling

- 200g cooked fresh or frozen gooseberries
- 3tbsp icing sugar
- 2tbsp lemon juice
- 200ml double cream

Pistachio Crunch

- 200g caster sugar
- 75g shelled pistachio nuts crushed

Method

Profiteroles

1. Pre heat oven 180°C Gas mark 5 and line a baking sheet with baking parchment.

2. Sift the flour onto a large sheet of paper.

3. Put the butter, milk, water, sugar and salt into a pan. Heat gently until the butter is melted. Increase the heat, bring to the boil. Remove pan from the heat and tip in all the flour. Beat the mixture to form a thick dough. Put pan back on a low heat, continue to beat the dough, for 1 minute. Remove and cool.

4. Gradually beat in the eggs, beating well until the dough is smooth and glossy.

5. Spoon the dough onto the baking sheet to make 8 profiteroles.

6. Bake for 20 – 25 minutes until the profiteroles are golden brown.

7. Remove from the oven and pierce the base of each, return to the oven for 5 minutes to dry out.

8. Cool on a wire rack while you make the filling and crunch.

9. Using a spoon or piping bag fitted with a nozzle, fill the centre of each choux bun with the gooseberry cream. Serve drizzled with melted white chocolate and small pieces of the crunch and add the remaining gooseberry sauce to the plate.

The Create & Cook Competition is a fun, innovative cookery competition for young cooks aged 12-14 in Hampshire secondary schools. It is run by fit2cook food education and sponsored by The Southern Co-operative. The aims of the Competition are to nurture young talent and celebrate local food. Young cooks have to design a two course menu using as many Hampshire ingredients as possible and they have to fill in a questionnaire about their local produce. This encourages them to think about how their food is produced and the advantages of buying local - sustainability, food miles and supporting local farmers and food producers. The Competition in Hampshire is supported by Hampshire Fare, Hampshire Farmers Markets, Lainston House Hotel, Newlyns Farm Cookery School and Highbury College. Now in its fifth year the Competition has discovered dozens of fantastic young cooks all with a passion for creating menus that have a flavour of where they live.

Chris is a student at Robert May's School, Odiham To find out more and how to enter the 2014 Competition please see www.fit2cook.co.uk/createandcook

Filling

1. Blend together the gooseberries, icing sugar, and lemon juice. Press through a sieve into a bowl.

2. Whip the cream until soft peaks, fold in 4 tbsp of gooseberry puree.

3. Using a spoon or piping bag fitted with a nozzle, fill the centre of each choux bun with the gooseberry cream.

Pistachio Crunch

. Line a baking sheet with baking parchment. Put sugar in a saucepan, put on to a medium heat, and melt the sugar slowly. When sugar is a nut brown colour remove from the heat, stir in the pistachios.

. Pour on to the baking sheet and leave to set. Crush when cold.

119

Ingredients

- 80zs Self Raising Flour
- 30zs Margarine
- 30zs Sugar
- 30zs Currants
- 10z peel or coconut
- 1 beaten egg with a little milk

Mary Wheeler's Rock Buns

Method

1. Rub margarine into flour, add sugar, currants, peel or coconut, mix well together with egg and milk.

2. Place rough heaps on baking tray. It makes about 12 cakes

3. Bake on a hot oven for 20 minutes

Mary Wheeler

Mary Wheeler was born in 1926 at Ripple near Deal to parents who worked on the land, her father's trade being a waggoner. During a period when her father was employed near Cranbrook, she met her husband, Ted, who also worked with horses, and they married later and their first child, Glenda was born in 1945. They moved onto Staplehurst where they worked on a mixed stock farm that also grew hops. Mary had a son 2 years later, in 1953 they moved to Preston where Ted took up a position as Shepherd, where he remained all his working life. 3 more children were born and family life was hard as there was no indoor plumbing but they were happy years. Mary was very fond of her garden and grew many prize winning flowers. She was very involved in village life as the years went by, helping out at the local school, flower shows and also organising socials and dances. As the years went by they moved to Wingham, near Canterbury to a bungalow, Mary loved her bungalow and soon had many friends calling in for tea and a good chat where she always had something tasty to serve them.

Ingredients

Panna cotta

- 200ml double cream
- 300ml buttermilk
- 125g sugar
- ½ vanilla pod
- Zest of half a lemon
- Juice of half a lemon
- 2 leaves of gelatine
- ½ cup of cold water

Honey roasted plums

- 100g dark brown sugar
- 2 large tablespoons clear honey
- 100g unsalted butter, cut into cubes
- A few sprigs of thyme
- 6 plums (ripe but firm), halved and pitted

Pistachio tuile

- 140g icing sugar
- 35g plain flour
- 35g unsalted butter
- 50ml orange juice
- 50g chopped pistachios

Vanilla And Buttermilk Panna Cotta With Marwells Honey Roasted Plums, Pistachio Tuile

Serves 4

Method

Panna Cotta
Preparation Time 30 minutes
Setting Time 4 hours

Remove the seeds from the vanilla pod and retain both. Place 100ml of double cream in a saucepan with the lemon zest, juice, sugar, vanilla pod and seeds. Slowly bring to boil over a gentle heat allowing the flavours to infuse into the cream. At the same time soak the gelatine in the cold water until soft. Take the pan off the heat. Squeeze out all of the water from the gelatine and dissolve into the warm cream mixture and allow to cool. Lightly whip the rest of the cream and set aside. Pass (sieve) the vanilla cream and gelatine mixture onto the buttermilk in a large mixing bowl and mix well, gently fold in the whipped cream. Pour into moulds (small pudding, dariole moulds or ramekin) and place in fridge to set.

oney Roasted Plums
eparation Time 10 minutes
ooking Time 10 minutes.
eheat an oven to 200°C. Melt the
utter with the honey, sugar and thyme
an ovenproof pan over a gentle heat.
urn up to a medium heat and cook
or 2 minutes, stirring continuously
he mixture will bubble vigorously
nd will be very hot, be careful not to
urn yourself). Add the halved plums,
ut side down and cook for a further
minutes. Turn the plums and place
he pan in the preheated oven and
oast until the caramel is deep brown
n colour (about 4 to 5 minutes). Allow
o cool slightly for a couple of minutes
hen serve.

Pistachio Tuile
Preparation Time 10 minutes
Cooking Time 5 minutes.
Preheat an oven to 200°C. Mix together
the icing sugar, flour, butter, orange
juice and pistachios, taking care not to
incorporate air into the mixture. Rest
the mixture in the fridge for couple of
hours if possible to allow the gluten to

relax. Line a baking tray with silicon
paper or baking paper. Spoon the
chilled mixture on to the sheet making
sure to leave room for them to spread
on the tray during cooking. Place in
oven and cook for 3 to 4 minutes or
until evenly coloured. Take out of
oven and allow to cool for a couple of
minutes then place each tuile over a
rolling pin to give them a curved shape.
When cooled completely place in an air
tight container ready for use.

To serve
1. Take the panna cotta out of the fridge
   and leave for two minutes to warm a
   little. Remove from the mould onto a
   clean dessert plate (you can run the
   side of the mould under warm water
   if it is stuck being careful not to get
   the panna cotta wet).

2. Spoon on the warm roasted plums
   and some of the syrup to the side of
   the panna cotta.

3. Place one of the tuiles on top of the
   panna cotta and serve.

Shepherds Delight Marmalade

Serves: 8 x 1 lb jars

Ingredients

- 3 pink grapefruit
- 3 blush or blood red oranges (whichever is in season)
- 2 large lemons
- 6 pints (approx 3 litres) water
- 5lb (2 1/2 kg) granulated sugar

Method

1. Preheat the oven to 170 °c/Gas mark 3 or simmering oven for the Aga.

2. Warm the sugar in the oven or put the sugar to warm at the back of the Aga (if using an Aga) as it will dissolve faster.

3. The easiest method is to soften the fruits first. Place the whole fruits (oranges, grapefruits and lemons) in a large saucepan and cover with 6 pints of water. Put the lid on and bring to the boil; once it has come to the boil, remove and place the pan in the oven for about 2hrs, or until the fruit has softened. Once softened, remove the fruit from the pan (but keep the pan and water as you need it later) and place in a colander. Leave to cool for about half an hour. When cool enough to handle, cut each fruit in half and scoop out the flesh, pips and pith. Using a small sharp serated knife, really scrape out any remaining white pith so that all you're left with is the rind.

4. Place all this fruity flesh back into the pan with the water. Bring to the boil for about 6 minutes, and then strain this through a nylon sieve, really pressing the pulp through the sieve using a wooden spoon. The pulp contains all the pectin which is needed to make the marmalade set, so it's important to squeeze through.

5. Cut the rind of the grapefruit, oranges and lemons into strips, either fine or chunky, depending on your preference. Place the pulpy liquid and rind into a preserving pan and add the sugar slowly until there are no remaining crystals. When completely dissolved, bring to the boil, and boil rapidly for about 10-15minutes, or until set. Leave in the pan for about 20 minutes (this prevents the rind from floating to the top). Pour into warm, prepared jars. Seal and label.

SHEPHERDS COURT
CHAWTON

Shepherds Court is a beautifully converted barn, offering Bed & Breakfast, situated on a 135 acre working sheep farm, within the South Downs National Park, between the historic Hampshire villages of Chawton and Selborne.

Furnished to a high standard of comfort and style Shepherds Court has been carefully converted to retain lots of traditional character & charm.

Guests can enjoy a farmhouse breakfast, cooked on the Aga. Locally sourced, farm assured, organic and fair-trade produce is used where possible with the emphasis always on serving delicious and good quality food.

Whatever the reason for being in this lovely part of rural England, whether it's business or pleasure, walking or cycling, visiting family or friends, a celebration or just an escape to the country, Shepherds Court offers a warm and friendly welcome to all.

125

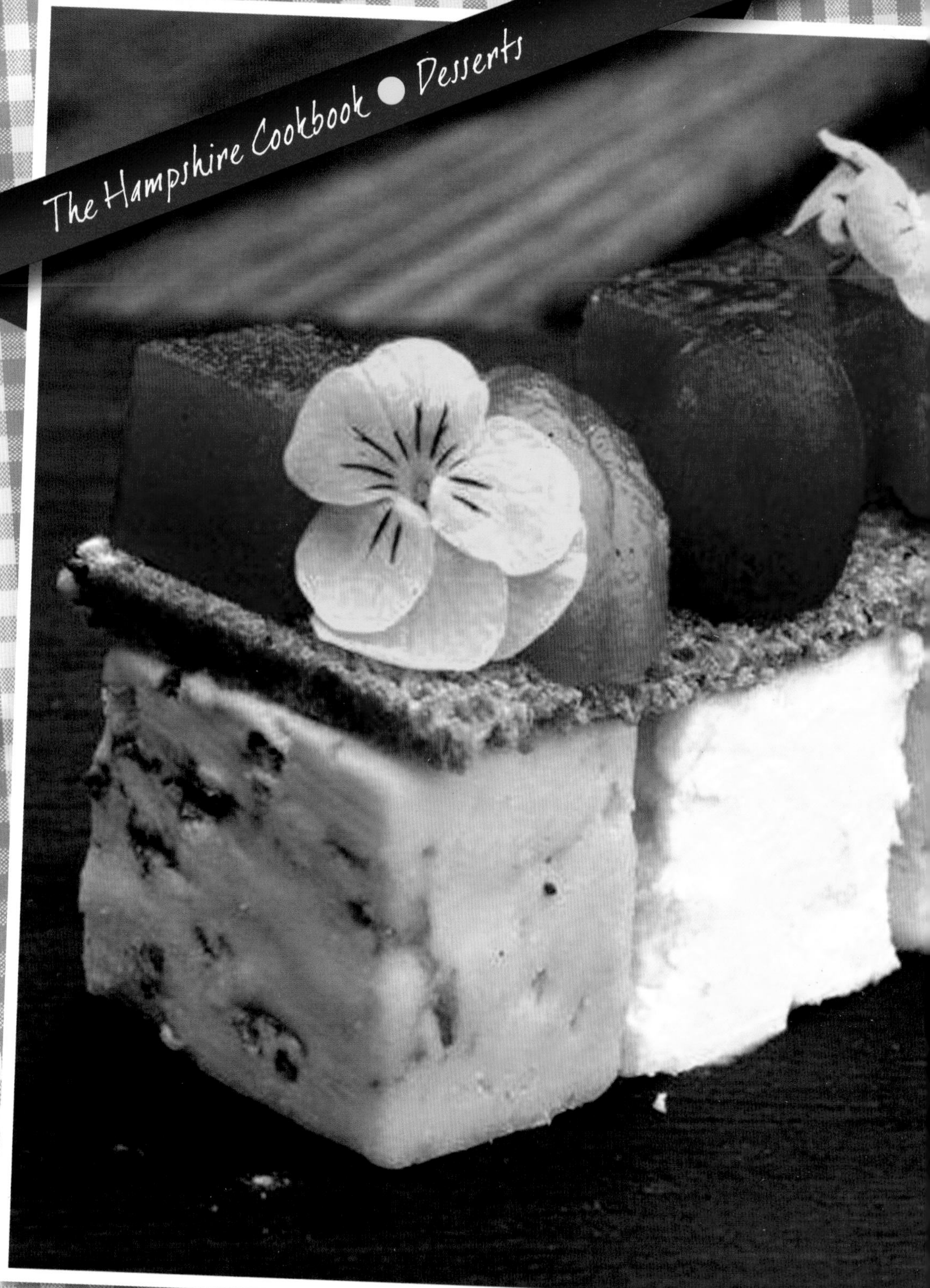

Harvest Fine Food's Local Cheeseboard

Loosehanger's Old Sarum
A delicious, creamy blue cheese judged 'Best Blue Cheese 2007'. Made with pure Ayrshire cow's milk to produce a wonderful velvety texture.

Rosary Goats
A creamy, moist and soft cheese with a light and fluffy texture made from pasteurised goat milk.

Tunwoth Soft
Made using unpasteurised cow milk and special cultures with traditional rennet, that when combined produces a creamy textured unique flavour with a distinctive wrinkled rind.

Lyburn's Old Winchester
A much dryer and harder cheese, with a nutty flavour, more like an Old Amsterdam.

Our cheeseboard is topped with crisp homemade rye bread, quince jelly, vanilla spiced apricots, black grapes and viola flowers.

Harvest Fine Foods is an independent, family-run business delivering a comprehensive range of fresh fruit and vegetables, dry stores, chilled and frozen foods to caterers throughout Hampshire. We pride ourselves in offering a comprehensive range of high quality products at very competitive prices.

At *Harvest Fine Foods* we share a passion for great food, and great dishes start with quality ingredients. Much of our time is spent sourcing new products and forging relationships with local artisan producers, growers and chefs. We feel our role is to provide a route to market for these wonderful products to our diverse customer base throughout Hampshire whilst allowing the producers to get on with what they do best. Of course, we are driven by customer demand and increasingly, chefs are putting local produce at the heart of their menus. Nothing gives us greater pleasure than seeing talented chefs create culinary masterpieces from quality local produce.

Rhubarb Souffle

Serves: 4
Preparation time:
40 minutes
Cooking time:
8 minutes

HOTEL
TERRAVINA

Method

Soufflé base (best prepared the night before):
Mix the water with the corn flour & add it to a saucepan with the other ingredients. Cook over a low heat for 10 to 15 minutes until the rhubarb is soft & then purée with a stick blender or smoothie maker. Pour this into a container & cover the surface with cling film to prevent a crust forming, then chill in the fridge overnight to cool & rest. This can be stored in the fridge for three days and will make a few batches.

Moulds:
Brush the inside of each soufflé mould with a thin, even layer of soft butter. Add a spoonful of the pain d'epices crumb & tap it around until the butter is completely coated. Pour out the excess crumb into the next butter lined mould and continue.

Soufflé mix:
Add the egg white & lemon juice to a mixing bowl. Whisk until the egg white starts to foam & then slowly pour the sugar into the bowl while whisking. Whisk until the mix reaches a soft peak. Add half of this mix to the soufflé base in a round bottom bowl & whisk them together to form an even colour. Add the second half & fold the mix in carefully until the colour is again consistent. Add the finished soufflé mix to a piping bag and pipe into the prepared moulds, making sure that the mix does not go above the lining.

Ingredients

Soufflé base:
- 500g forced/pink rhubarb, roughly chopped
- 50g castor sugar
- 150ml cold water
- 35g corn flour

Moulds:
- Soft butter
- Pain d'epices crumb, fine & dry

Soufflé mix (to serve 4):
- 100g egg white
- 2 drops of lemon juice
- 150g castor sugar
- 100g soufflé base

To cook:
The soufflé can be stored in the fridge for up to an hour or maybe more if the mixture is stable. Cook from the fridge, on a tray, in a pre-heated oven at 180°C for approximately 8 minutes, turning halfway. Serve immediately with clotted cream or an ice cream of your choice and enjoy!

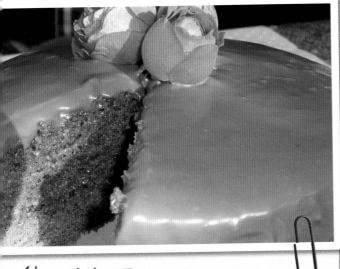

New Forest
Chocolates

Chocolate Fudge Cake with Ganache Icing

Serves: 8 plus spare for the next day

Method

1 Heat your oven to 170 deg C, 325 deg F or Gas mark 3.

2 Line the base of two 20cm (8 inch) round cake tins with baking parchment and brush the insides and base with a little sunflower oil.

3. Sift the flour, cocoa powder and baking powder into a bowl. Add the margarine, sugar, vanilla essence and eggs.

4. Beat all the ingredients together, ideally with an electric hand whisk, until the mixture is thick and creamy. Don't over beat as it might start to separate.

5. Put half of the mixture into each of the cake tins and put them on the middle shelf of the oven. Bake for 40 to 45 minutes.

6. Let them cool in the tins for five minutes before taking them out to fully cool on a rack.

7. For the icing, heat the cream in a saucepan or microwaveable jug until close to boiling (but not boiling as you might scorch the chocolate). Pour over the chocolate, leave it to settle for a few seconds and then stir. As if by magic the cream and chocolate will suddenly stir together into a beautiful creamy dark brown ganache.

8. Let it cool and then place in the fridge. Stir the icing a few times while in the fridge.

9 If you cannot wait, eat the warm cake using this ganache icing as a warm pouring sauce. Perfect with a drizzle of locally produced double cream.

10. If you have more will-power, wait until the ganache icing has thickened in the fridge.

11. When it is like soft butter, spread a third of the icing on one cake, put the other cake on top and cover the top with the rest of the icing and let it drizzle down the sides.

Ingredients

- Sunflower oil
- 250g (8oz) self raising flour
- 6 tablespoons fair-trade cocoa powder (or drinking chocolate if you want the cake to be a little milder)
- 2 teaspoons baking powder
- 300g (10oz) softened sunflower or baking margarine (not low fat spread)
- 300g (10oz) fair-trade soft brown sugar
- 2 teaspoons of fair-trade vanilla essence
- 6 large free range Hampshire eggs

300g (half pint) Hampshire double cream

- 300 g (10oz) dark or milk chocolate, supplied by New Forest Chocolates* or use any other good quality chocolate that you like

129

Ingredients

- 24oz unsalted butter
- 10oz cocoa powder
- 1.2 1itres cream
- 4oz icing sugar
- 11 oz dark chocolate
- 11 oz white chocolate
- 16egg yolks
- 20oz caster sugar
- 2 cups roasted hazelnuts

Chocolate Marquise Mix

Method

1. Melt butter and add cocoa
2. Mix cream and icing sugar to soft peak.
3. Melt dark and white chocolate.
4. Whisk egg yolks and caster sugar until stiff.
5. Add chocolate mixture and then butter mixture Fold in cream mixture and the hazelnuts.
6. Pour into a mould and allow to set in the fridge.

The Hermitage Restaurant has been integral to The Brookfield Hotel's success for many years.

Seating up to 120 people for a formal banquet, it is also a delightful venue for more relaxed occasions, such as family celebrations and business successes.

The spacious restaurant, overlooking the gardens, offers a regularly changing Table d'hote menu, while snacks and bar meals are available from the bar and adjoining lounge.

Sunday lunch is popular with local residents and visitors alike; our 2-course weekday lunch is so popular it has to be booked in advance, to be certain of obtaining a table.

Wine tasting dinners, fish suppers and themed evenings are all held regularly.

Working breakfasts, morning coffee, lunch, afternoon tea and dinner are all well catered for by The Brookfield kitchens, presided over by our popular head chef, whilst our restaurant and bar manager is always happy to recommend a suitable wine to enhance your dining experience.

Jenkyn's Vineyard

Jenkyn Place 2009 Brut

The near perfect growing season of 2009 has produced a Jenkyn Place Cuvée which in many ways represents a true single vineyard wine. The wine is fascinatingly complex, yet quite simple at the same time. The core of ripe, creamy orchard fruit is very much in the background. The driving characteristic of the wine is one of distinct mineral energy – a flint-like 'terroir' character which suggests a vineyard coming of age and reaching a very particular expression in what was an exceptional vintage. The high balancing acidity will ensure that this wine will continue to age brilliantly for many years to come. This is the best Jenkyn Place Cuvée to date. Yet it does not just need to be drunk for toasts and with canapés, but in fact The Sommelier Wine Awards 2013 awarded it a Gold Medal and Top Wine for food match with fish and chips. Price - £24.99 (case discount available)

Jenkyn Place 2009 Rosé

The 2009 vintage was one of the best ever and we kept back the ripest of the Pinot Noir for late picking at Jenkyn Place. We could have made a very decent red wine – in fact we did – but solely to make this Rosé. The initial gently tannic structure of the wine in its early stages has given way to reveal a harmonious pallet of wild strawberry and cherry, with notes of jasmine and violet emerging after some time in the glass. After four years the wine is just coming into its own and promises to develop even more detail and nuance in years to come. The 2008 vintage won Five Stars for food matching with Strawberries and Cream in the 2012 What Food What Wine competition.Price - £24.99 (case discount available). To buy please contact Simon Bladon simon@jenkynplace.com or visit our website www.jenkynplace.com.

Directory

Alice Lisle
Rockford Green
Ringwood
Hampshire
BH24 3NA
01425 474700
alicelisle@fullers.co.uk

Bat and Ball
Hyden Farm Lane
Clanfield
Waterlooville
Hampshire
PO8 0UB
023 92632692
batandball@fullers.co.uk

The Bear and Ragged Staff
Stonymarsh
Romsey
SO51 0LB
01794 368602
info@thebearandragged
staff.net

Cams Mill
Cams Mill
The Square
Bishop's Waltham

Southampton
Hampshire
SO32 1AF
01489 893 350
crowninnmanager.
bishopswaltham@fullers.co.uk

Forest Holidays' Blackwood Forest Cabins
Larkwhistle Farm Road
Micheldever
Winchester
Hampshire
SO21 3BG
0845 130 8223
info@forestholidays.co.uk

The Good Life Farm Shop
Springvale Road
Headbourne
Worthy
Winchester
Hampshire
SO23 7LD
01962 889000

Grey Hound
46 Winchester Street
Overton
Basingstoke

Hampshire
RG25 3HS
01256 770241

Horse and Groom
2 Broad Street
Alresford
Winchester
Hampshire
SO24 9AQ
01962 734 809
horseandgroom@fullers.co.uk

Kings Head
The Square
Wickham
Fareham
Hampshire
PO17 5JN
01329 832123 (3079)
kingshead.fareham@fullers.co.uk

Links Tavern
Portsmouth Road
Liphook
Hampshire
GU30 7EF
01428 723773
Links@fullers.co.uk

New Forest Hotel

Lyndhurst Road
Ashurst
Hampshire
SO40 7AA
02380 292721

Oak Inn

Pinkney Lane
Bank
Lyndhurst
Hampshire
SO43 7FD
02380 282350
OakInn@fullers.co.uk

Old Custom House

Vernon Building
Gunwharf Quays
Portsmouth
Hampshire
PO1 3TY
023 92832333
OldCustomsHouse@fullers.co.uk

The Pelican

Asa House
Tanshire Park
Shackleford Road
Elstead
GU8 6LB

01252 705219
simona@pelicanbuying.co.uk

Pilgrims Inn

Hythe Road
Marchwood
Southampton
Hampshire
SO40 4WU
02380 867752
pilgriminn@fullers.co.uk

Red Lion

Chalton
Waterlooville
Hampshire
PO8 0BG
023 92592246
redlion.chalton@fullers.co.uk

Ship Inn

Langstone Road
Langstone
Havant
Hampshire
PO9 1RD
023 92471719
Ship.Langstone@fullers.co.uk

Still and West

Bath Square
Old Portsmouth

Hampshire
PO1 2JL
023 92821567
stillandwest@fullers.co.uk

White Buck Inn

Bisterne Close
Burley
Hampshire
BH24 4AZ
01425 402264
whitebuckinnmanager@
fullers.co.uk

White Hart

High Street
Stockbridge
Winchester
Hampshire
SO20 6HF
01264 810663
WhiteHart.Stockbridge-
Manager@fullers.co.uk

Wykeham Arms

75 Kingsgate Street
Winchester
Hampshire
SO23 9PE
01962 853834
wykehamarms@fullers.co.uk

The Team hcr

When our team of seven first met, we knew we wanted to create something that could help make a real difference to people's lives but we had no idea of the journey ahead.

Many months of hard work and excitement later and we are able to launch The Hampshire Cookbook - a project we are all incredibly proud to have been a part of.

The Prince's Trust Million Makers Challenge gave us the perfect excuse to work together and turn something we all felt passionate about into a profitable mini enterprise - feeding the proceeds back so that they can be used to help young people across the UK.

Right across our team, we have two things in common. We work for HCR, whose head office is in Hampshire. And we all love food. So, we put the two together.

This is a wonderfully understated county. We don't shout enough about our local produce. But you only have to look at the popularity of farmers markets here to understand how important locally produced food and drink are to the people who live in Hampshire.

Our team has worked hard to design a product that is unique and has never been done before. It has generated a real buzz - no doubt due to the extraordinary generosity of the book's contributors, including a number of world famous cooks and chefs.

During this very special project, we have been able to harness our creativity whilst supporting The Prince's Trust - a rewarding experience for all of us.

On behalf of the team, I would like to thank everyone involved - including HCR and the many local businesses who supported us along the way. And thank you for buying The Hampshire Cookbook. It features some truly mouthwatering recipes - now enjoy!

Simon Hood
The Hampshire Cookbook
Head of Marketing

The Hampshire Cookbook team is made up of

Simon Hood
Jack Miller
Alex Birt
Emma Farebrother
Liz Taylor
Nicky Bond
Lisa Mattock

Thank you!

The entire team would like to thank the following people who have helped make this project possible and supported us along the way.

- Our friends, family and everyone from HCR
- Hampshire's Farmers Markets
- Hampshire Fare
- Paul Hollywood
- Simon Rogan
- Delia Smith
- Rick Stein
- Marcus Wareing
- Tommy Miah
- Eric Lanlard
- Antonio Carluccio
- Dean Chillmaid for all his patience, help and support throughout this long process
- David Kimber for his great support, advice and keeping us on the right path!
- The Prince's Trust
- Fullers and all our sponsors

And more importantly you for buying our book!